Milton's Paradise Lost

Peter Davies

GREENWICH EXCHANGE
LONDON

Greenwich Exchange, London

Milton's
Paradise Lost
©Peter Davies 2010

First published in Great Britain in 2010
All rights reserved

This book is sold subject to the conditions that it shall not, by way of trade or otherwise, be lent, resold, hired out or otherwise circulated without the publisher's prior consent in any form of binding or cover other than that in which it is published and without a similar condition including this condition being imposed on the subsequent purchaser.

Printed and bound by **imprint**digital.net
Typesetting and layout by Jude Keen, London
Tel: 020 8355 4541
Cover design by December Publications, Belfast
Tel: 028 90286559
Cover © The Courtauld Gallery, London

Greenwich Exchange Website: www.greenex.co.uk

Cataloguing in Publication Data available from the British Library

ISBN: 978-1-906075-47-7

For Justine Cohen

Contents

	Preface	9
1	Milton: The Man and His Epic	11
2	Satan and the Rebel Angels	20
3	The Ethos of Heaven	43
4	Adam and Eve in Eden	55
5	The Fall	64
6	Aftermath	79
7	The Poetry of *Paradise Lost*	86
8	Critical Fortunes	94
	Further Reading	103

Preface

The quatercentenary of Milton's birth in 2008 prompted a flurry of publications on the man and his works, ranging from newspaper articles to full-scale critical biographies. This was no bad thing for a poet who has always seemed to need his advocates – the flurry was, after all, the merest trickle compared to the attention Shakespearean anniversaries generate.

Most, though not all, of this output was in the nature of things laudatory. Anniversaries of great figures tend to lead to a willingness to suspend the critical faculties. Still, it is comforting to see that individual books of *Paradise Lost*, the work above all others by which Milton's stature must be judged, are still taught for public examination purposes in schools. Whether their treatment there, under such prescriptive headings as 'pastoral' or 'gothic', is helpful to understanding is questionable. It encourages a dip-in and dip-out approach that suggests a shying away from a desire to engage with Milton's central themes in the poem. Books I and II, which feature Satan in his pomp, remain by far the most popular. One wonders how many students are likely to sit down and read the entire twelve.

When *Paradise Lost* made its first appearance in ten books in 1667 Milton's reputation was in eclipse. Its austerely republican author, who had been a fierce apologist for regicide and a diligent servant of parliamentary government, had since 1660 lived at the mercy of a restored monarchy and its acolytes at court. At the Restoration his books had been publicly burnt by the hangman and he had been arrested and imprisoned for three months. After that he lived in obscurity.

It was an inauspicious time for Milton's epic. Literary tastes were changing. The temper of the age was one of irreverence and levity. Facile witticism was preferred to metaphysical wit. The attractively accessible work of John Dryden, who became poet laureate in 1668 and was also a popular playwright, was steering poetic forms away from the blank verse that had been the vehicle for the dramas of Shakespeare and the Jacobeans, and which Milton had insisted on as his medium for *Paradise Lost*. Glorying in the "reform of our numbers" which he ascribed to Sir John Denham (1615-69) and Edmund Waller (1606-87), hardly major poets, Dryden was the apostle of the rhyming couplet, which was to establish itself as the preponderant medium for heroic verse in the following century. This was to give poetry a completely different 'feel' from the sometimes difficult cragginess, in both form and thought, of an epic like *Paradise Lost*.

Yet there was enough memory of past glories left in the reading public of the Restoration period for Milton's epic to be recognised as the master work it is. Denham himself is popularly supposed to have entered the House of Commons in the autumn of 1667, waving one of its sheets still "wet from the press" and to have announced to astonished members that it was "part of the noblest poem that was ever wrote in any language or any age". Reading it in 1668, Sir John Hobart, who had been an MP under Cromwell and was to be one again under Charles II, pronounced it "not only above all modern attempts in verse, but equal to all the ancient poets".

From the moment of its publication *Paradise Lost* did well. The sums Milton received for it, probably amounting to less than £20, seem paltry, but the era of commercial authorship as we know it was still distant. *Paradise Lost* sold somewhere around 1,300 copies in its first year of publication and in excess of 3,000 within ten years, making it by the standards of the day, a popular work. Dryden paid Milton the compliment of making a version of it, entitled *The State of Innocence and Fall of Man*, for the operatic stage. His effort still makes an instructive comparison when read alongside Milton's. It was never performed, but Dryden's easygoing verse ensured great popularity for the printed version.

In the meantime Milton was encouraged to the production of a further, short, epic, *Paradise Regained* and the verse drama *Samson Agonistes* (both 1671). *Paradise Lost*'s second edition appeared in 1674. Books VII and X had been divided to give it the twelve books with which we are familiar. By this time his rehabilitation was assured and the edition was accompanied by two commendatory poems. Since that time Milton's critical reputation has endured its fluctuations, but his masterpiece has never stopped selling.

1

Milton: The Man and His Epic

By the time Milton came to the composition of *Paradise Lost* he had lived a life of deep study, travel and scholarship which had prepared him extraordinarily for such a major undertaking. His years as a scholar and poet had been largely very private ones, devoted to the development of his mind and the pursuit of his own concerns. There then succeeded a long period in which he turned his back on literary composition, emerging from the study into the public domain, and devoting all his powers to public service as Latin secretary to Oliver Cromwell and propagandist in English and Latin, first for the parliamentary Commonwealth regime, then for its successor, the Cromwell Protectorate. He wrestled for a time with the notion that Latin in which he was a fluent writer – and which was the international diplomatic language of the day – would have been the more natural vehicle for a work like *Paradise Lost*. We can only be thankful that he abandoned the idea.

Much of Milton's political propaganda was by its very nature ephemeral. Other parts of this output, ranging from such subjects as Church government, through attacks on censorship in publishing, to attempts to reformulate a workable system for parliamentary democracy, even with Cromwell dead and the future King Charles virtually at the gates, are great hammer blows in defence of the freedoms we regard as our right today.

The dogmatic tone of these majestic tracts tends to present Milton to us as more admirable than likeable. A man with such an unassailable sense of his own rectitude is always liable to come over as a prig. And it is unfortunate that the known facts of his life – especially his private life – have conspired to make Milton one of the least loved of England's major literary figures.

At Cambridge, where he was studious, proud, conscious of his merits if others were not, rebellious and contemptuous of a series of tutors, he had been known as the "Lady of Christ's" because of his great personal beauty. Physically handsome he may have been, but he was certainly never a ladies' man. The apparent facts of his first marriage, contracted in 1642 when he was in his early thirties to a young woman of 17, Mary Powell, have made him an easy butt of mirth down the ages. It seems that his wedding night was not a success. For a man of his times he does seem to have had extraordinarily little experience of these things. In any event his wife left him after a month and returned home to her parents.

But the facts of this misfortune have 'stuck' in the sense that they have given the impression that he did not – actually could not – really like women. Or that he could only like an idealised sort of woman, such as the Lady in *Comus* nursing a bloodless chastity, or a submissive, insipidly dutiful Eve. It overlooks the fact that Milton actually behaved with great generosity to his first wife and her family. When she returned to him in 1645 he did not spurn her. When in the following year the Powell family, who were Royalists, found themselves ejected from their Oxford home following the King's defeats, this die-hard republican unhesitatingly took them in under his roof.

The notion that Milton lacked a faculty of sensuous comprehension of women, or that he never experienced the pleasure of mental and emotional closeness to a woman, is surely not sustainable. Could the poet who in *Paradise Lost* makes Adam say to his fallen Eve,

> How can I live without thee! how forgo
> Thy sweet converse, and love so dearly joined,
>
> (IX, 908-9)

really never have known intimacy? Milton may have got off on the wrong foot in his first marriage. His impassioned poetic tribute to his second wife, Katherine Woodcock (who, like his first, had died in childbirth) "Methought I saw my late espoused saint" indicates that with a little encouragement this difficult man, who always expected more from anyone than they could deliver, was quite capable of being an uxorious husband.

By 1641 when Milton embarked on his career as a propagandist he had a substantial career as a poet behind him. I am not competent to judge his early Latin poems, but their translation by William Cowper (a happy choice) gives some idea of their grace (and their author's susceptibility to women). The beautiful, youthful ode 'On the Morning of Christ's Nativity' (1629); the enduringly lovely *L'Allegro* and *Il Penseroso* (c. 1632, not published until 1645); the masque *Comus* (performed at Ludlow Castle in 1634) and the immortal elegy 'Lycidas' (1638) had won him a substantial reputation.

Not long after the publication of 'Lycidas' he left for Italy, returning the following year to find his country on the eve of cataclysmic events. He thought to bury his head in the obscurity of a private school, but he was soon to be caught up and swept away in political affairs that called out to his deepest convictions. For the next twenty years, his sonnets apart, his poetic voice was effectively silent.

These are the years of *The Reason of Church Government Urged against Prelaty* (1642). This is the Presbyterian Milton's attack on the episcopalian High Church system governed by the Crown and tended by Charles I's Archbishop of Canterbury, William Laud, whose attempt to impose the Anglican prayer book on the Presbyterian Lowland Scots had effectively triggered the Civil War. It is followed by the provocative *The Doctrine and Discipline of Divorce* (1643). This is a personal reaction from a man still raw from his desertion by his wife. Yet in its insistence that incompatibility should be the principal basis for divorce, it comes over as strangely modern in anticipating the "irretrievable breakdown of marriage" of our times as the only ground for divorce, after centuries in which courts required proof of 'criminal' activity from one or other of the parties (for long, usually the woman). *Areopagitica* (1644), Milton's impassioned and persuasively crafted defence of the right to publish without the interference of government, is his greatest prose utterance and one whose relevance will never become redundant in any sovereign state, in any age.

During the King's trial, in January 1649, Milton was busy writing *The Tenure of Kings and Magistrates* which urged the lawfulness, from a people's point of view, of bringing to account "a tyrant or wicked king". Though it is not one of his most coherent works, it nevertheless states lucidly enough his position on tyranny. Echoes of it are to be heard in *Paradise Lost*.

To set out objections to the unlawful exercise of autocratic power while a king was alive was one thing (though *The Tenure* did not actually appear until after Charles' death). The period after the execution of Charles on 30th January 1649 compelled Milton as a servant of the republican regime to the defence of the act itself, something which could never be made popular with the people. His *Eikonoklastes* (The Iconoclast) was written by order of Parliament and published that October as an answer to *Eikon Basilike* (The King's Image) a work supposedly written by Charles, which had at a stroke managed to turn a selfish and inept despot into a man of almost saintly dignity. Milton's riposte and defence of regicide in the government's name is unworthy of his intellect in its opinions and arguments and was bound to be a failure in terms of public sentiment. Whatever his previous treachery and cruelties Charles had, at the end, simply behaved with too much dignity on the scaffold to be able to be 'written down' in this way – and all the world knew it. Men still believed in God. And if Parliament – and certainly Milton – vehemently dissented from Charles' claim to rule by divine right, it was a sentiment which still found plenty of resonance with ordinary people.

As the poet Andrew Marvell was to concede of Charles – and at that in a poem ostensibly praising Cromwell, 'An Horatian Ode upon Cromwell's Return from Ireland' (1650):

> He nothing common did or mean
> Upon that memorable scene:
>   But with his keener eye
>   The axe's edge did try:
> Nor called the gods with vulgar spite
> To vindicate his helpless right,
>   But bowed his comely head,
>   Down as upon a bed.

It was too resounding a testimony to the fallen king's nobility to be undermined by a pamphlet of near scurrility such as *Eikonoklastes*. It was also a remarkable testimony to the tolerance of the new regime that it could allow Marvell to get away with such sentiments – and to Milton's goodness of heart that in 1653 he recommended that the writer of what amounted to a civilised rebuke to his own 'public' performance should be given employment alongside him as one of Cromwell's Latin secretaries.

Milton ploughed on, producing propaganda to order in the service of the regime in which he had invested so much mental and moral capital. From 1649 until Cromwell's death in 1658, he was the apologist for a regicide government, and took on the supporters of the future Charles II (in exile on the Continent), who were assiduous in sowing the seeds for his return through such publications as *Defensio Regia pro Carolo I*, in whose composition the executed King's son had employed the celebrated French scholar Salmasius. In three works, *Defensio pro Populo Anglicano* (Defence of the English people, 1651), *Defensio Secunda* (1654) and *Defensio pro Se* (1655) Milton stuck to the thankless task of vindicating the Commonwealth's actions, and his own part in them, against criticism launched from across the Channel, in arguments which all too often do him no credit, descending as they frequently do to the level of mere abuse.

We imagine that he was probably also at work around this time on the comprehensive exposition in Latin of theological doctrine which is generally attributed to him, *De Doctrina Christiana*. It was lost and not found until 1823 when it surfaced among a bundle of papers in the Old State Paper Office in the Middle Treasury Gallery in Whitehall. An edition in English first appeared in 1825. *De Doctrina* sets forth many aspects of Christian belief that are specific to Milton, some of which emerge at moments in *Paradise Lost*.

De Doctrina apart, there is a sense of huge futility about these years of Milton's life with their expenditure of such great capacities on such mean ends. But Milton, as surely as any of the great crusading journalists of modern times, passionately believed in the power of the written word to secure change for good. He believed in Eternity, but he had also been equally sure that God somehow had a special purpose for "his Englishmen" on this earth. And that purpose was surely to be rooted in republican government in politics and an egalitarian Presbyterian government of the Church.

With Oliver Cromwell dead, his son Richard who had succeeded him deposed, and the imminent arrival of Charles Stuart to claim the throne of England, Milton is still at it, desperately trying to breathe life into a morally bankrupt government in such a suicidally courageous pamphlet as *The Ready and Easy Way to Establish a Free Commonwealth* (1660). Blind long since, and as a result compelled to relinquish his full-time duties as the government's diplomatic secretary, Milton is by this point so out of touch with the political realities that he dedicates *The Ready and Easy Way* to General Monck, completely unaware that the great Commonwealth general has for some months been in secret negotiations with the representatives of Charles Stuart.

Monck's reward for the restoration of the monarchy was to be created Duke of Albermarle. At the end of twenty years of the most dramatic revolution in England since the Conquest, Milton was left with the utter defeat of all his most cherished political and religious ideas. King and Episcopalian Church were in triumph, and he must creep home to his London house and hope not to attract the notice of those who had been galled by his asperity and might be thirsty for revenge. What he had not lost, remarkably since his project for the realisation of God's kingdom on earth had collapsed completely, was his faith in God and his desire to express that through his artistic creativity.

Although Milton was primarily engaged in political journalism during these years, we know that he had been thinking sporadically about writing an epic poem at some future date. We do not know at what point he actually began to compose it. In the preface to Book II of *The Reason of Church Government*, he had glanced aside from his major thesis to discuss what form this epic might take. It might be "diffuse" as he put it, that is on a large canvas such as Homer or Virgil employed, or "brief" in which category he included the Old Testament's Book of Job. He had, we know, seriously considered an Arthurian epic. We can be thankful that he did not act on the idea. A Miltonic version of Tennyson's much later *Idylls of the King* does not bear thinking about. Arthur and his paladins were simply not fundamental enough as a subject to enable him to mine his most deeply held beliefs. Or, as C.S. Lewis puts it in *A Preface to Paradise Lost* (1942), had he chosen Arthur as his subject "Spenserian Milton might have grown to full development and the actual Milton, the 'Miltonic' Milton, would have been repressed." Certainly, to have elevated the Arthurian legend to a plane where it could carry the weight of metaphysical significance for which he strove, Milton might well have found himself bogged down in allegory. As we shall see, the brief intrusion of allegory into *Paradise Lost* is not a successful one.

The other option was a tragedy. According to Milton's nephew Edward Phillips in his *Life of Milton* (1694), his uncle had told him that what is now Satan's opening speech in the early part of Book IV, "O thou that with surpassing glory crowned ... ", had originally been intended as the opening lines of a tragedy. We know that Shakespeare's *Macbeth*, and its study of the invigorating power of evil, had a deep interest for him. Again, given the type of poetry he was to choose as the vehicle for his ideas, we can be glad, too, that this did not happen. God, Satan, Heaven, Hell, Adam, Eve, Paradise, the Fall, may have been the hugest and most fraught with difficulty of all the subjects he might have chosen, but it was the theme with which his uncompromising nature was most at one.

There has been a tendency in modern criticism, particularly though not exclusively in America, to seem to hanker after a return to a position that sees *Paradise Lost* as some kind of sermon or at least as an unswerving statement of Milton's religious beliefs. Given the great marshalling of ideas in which its author had been involved for years as he embarked on it, it would not perhaps be surprising that we should go to it expecting an exposition of those ideas. But in adopting that expectation we are in danger of forgetting that the author of *Paradise Lost* was writing as a poet, not as the author of *The Reason of Church Government, Areopagitica* or *The Tenure of Kings and Magistrates*, even granted that moments from these prose works do occasionally surface as angry squibs in the epic.

Milton of course does not make life any easier for himself by stating at the outset that the aim of his poem is to "justify the ways of God to men". It is not a position which appears to leave the poet or the reader much room for manoeuvre. As a pamphleteer and propagandist Milton was a writer of consummate skill in giving shape to ideas on religion, politics and social issues about which he had thought long and deeply. But let him loose as a poet and unsuspected, contradictory, not to say insurrectionary, emotions may be seen to be finding their way to the surface. Authority – even that proceeding from God? – may suddenly be seen as demeaning to the human spirit; woman, the biddable helpmeet, finds transfiguration as sex goddess and enslaver of nature; obedience suddenly becomes less attractive than the intelligent exercise of the will.

To take an obvious parallel, when Shakespeare embarked on his second trilogy of historical plays, the two parts of *King Henry IV* and *King Henry V*, he may well have set out, especially under the watchful gaze of Queen Elizabeth I and her ministers, to demonstrate the beneficent effects of firm government, and to explore the difficult nature of responsible kingship. And such themes will doubtless form the subject of student essays and inform productions of these plays for years to come. But the fact is that Falstaff, the Lord of Misrule, inconveniently steals the show, even down to the mere handful of lines which so beautifully and memorably report his death in *King Henry V*. After his departure from the scene in the opening phases of that play there is little left to Shakespeare but patriotic pageantry and jingoistic bombast, stirring though they may be in a limited sort of way.

The great works of literature have a habit of taking on an autonomous life, no matter how firm the hand that guides them. Do we anywhere feel the presence of Homer or his opinions in the *Iliad*? No. The petulance of Agamemnon, the splenetic pride of Achilles and the motherly concern and wifely fears of Andromache are imbued with a truth to reality that operates outside any framework of authorial moral imperatives that we can sense. Or, to bring ourselves some twenty-seven centuries forward from Homer to such a completely different kind of work as James Joyce's novel *Ulysses* and put the question another way: is the author's use of the guiding framework of the *Odyssey* – which may well have kept him on track from a structural point of view, yet which so many critics make germane to an understanding of the book – in any sense necessary to what we experience as we encounter the three-dimensional physical vividness and the mental vitality of Leopold and Molly Bloom? The answer is surely not.

Milton was a moralist. But when he writes as a poet unforeseen things are likely to happen. To write *Paradise Lost* he had to assemble a cast of characters, each of whom presented a formidable proposition. Having done this he then had to manoeuvre them through a theological landscape whose terrain was, somewhat perilously for him as a servant of God as well as a poet, apparently undeviatingly mapped out for him in the Bible.

For a man addressing himself to a Christian readership it was a daunting task, and in embarking on reading our own way through it, we might well wonder how he was to navigate his poetic voyage and come safe into port without losing a few men overboard on the way. But, as we do when we read Homer, we can only judge the behaviour of these characters – gods, angels or heroes though they may be – as we find them on the page, without preconceptions about the way they ought to be behaving, given their rank and responsibilities in the scheme of things. We shall find that we extract most from *Paradise Lost* if we set out not to listen for what we think are Milton's intentions for this cast of exalted beings, but to hearken instead to the sometimes surprising results of the free play of a poetic imagination which, when moral restraints on it are allowed to fall away, thrills to a sensuous delight in the people and things of this world. In other words, what really matters is not what Milton *meant* to happen, but the much more exciting, more rewarding question of what actually *does* happen in *Paradise Lost*.

2

Satan and the Rebel Angels

The personality of Satan dominates the first two books of *Paradise Lost*. He has their finest speeches. He makes an indelible impression on all those around him in the poem – and on us the readers. It is possible to feel that in these two books he establishes such a lead in dominance, makes such claims on us as a character, autonomous in strength of purpose and wholly understandable in motive, that he is never thereafter overhauled by any other of the poem's dramatis personae.

How can this be allowed to happen? we ask – especially in a poem whose avowed aim is to justify the ways of God to men. The formula that has so often been used to explain the difficulty is that Satan must be seen to be a worthy adversary to God, whose plans for a new race of beings living in a peaceful Paradise as an 'alternative' Heaven after the Fall of the rebel angels, he after all comprehensively wrecks in the poem. He cannot be seen to bring about these far-reaching ends merely as a common villain. He must be mighty so that his final defeat, some time in the future at the hands of God/the Messiah can be savoured in all its beneficent magnitude.

There seems to me to be something fundamentally wrong with an argument such as this. Satan could, after all, have been made a figure of destructive power without having been made at the same time in the slightest bit attractive, much less imbued with a quality of nobility, as he undoubtedly is. This is a being "Who durst defy th' Omnipotent to arms" (I, 49), and whatever we may think of the wisdom of such a proceeding, it is undeniably a project of awesome courage and daring.

Yet, interestingly, when Satan does make his entrance to the poem (I, 34) it is merely as "Th' infernal Serpent" of Genesis, a state to which Milton will return him in Book X when he returns to Pandemonium to report back to the assembled devils on the success of his mission against mankind. If this was a slip of the pen, or simply something to which an adherence to Genesis compelled him, Milton immediately corrects himself to adjust the effect of this first impression. Satan is never thereafter mentioned in Books I and II except in terms of respect that remind us that he was once a chief among archangels. For Milton he is always "Arch-Enemy" (I, 81), "Arch-Fiend" (I, 156) or "Lost Archangel" (I, 243). To his second-in-command Beëlzebub he is still "Chief of many throned Powers" (I, 128) and "Leader of those armies bright/Which, but th' Omnipotent, none could have foiled!" (I, 272-3). To the rebel angels, flung into the Abyss and now rallying their stunned senses as they make their way over the burning lake to answer his powerful summons, "Awake, arise, or be for ever fallen!" (I, 330), he is still "Their great Commander" (I, 358).

And remarkably, having been only nine days before

> Hurled headlong flaming from th' ethereal sky,
> With hideous ruin and combustion, down
> To bottomless perdition, there to dwell
> In adamantine chains and penal fire
>
> (I, 45-8)

– a punishment with which Milton batters its hapless recipient (and us the readers) with poetry of well-nigh percussive force, Satan is almost immediately active in his exertions to rally the troops. Their misfortunes notwithstanding, Beëlzebub is reminded that he is (or has only very recently been)

> he whom mutual league,
> United thoughts and counsels, equal hope
> And hazard in the glorious enterprise
> Joined with me once.
>
> (I, 87-90)

It is a nicely judged appeal, reminding Beëlzebub as it does of his recent participation in the risk assessment that presumably took place when he joined the revolt in the first place.

We at this stage of course don't know what the specific cause of Satan's revolt was. The Bible is of little help here. It only tells us that there was a war in Heaven involving a third of the angelic host (Revelation 12:3-9) and that Satan "was cast out into the earth, and all his angels were cast out with him". It is not until Book V that the Archangel Raphael will reveal Satan's *casus belli*. His account will of course ascribe the basest of motives to Satan – but that is the privilege of a victor.

The opening of Book I conveys a powerfully anguished sense in Milton of overwhelming and universal *loss* in the events he is about to relate – a sense of loss that, interestingly, seems to be extended to Satan:

> the thought
> Both of lost happiness and lasting pain
> Torments him
>
> (I, 54-6)

no less than to mankind's first representatives, who have been induced by him

> in that happy state,
> Favoured of Heaven so highly, to fall off
> From their Creator, and transgress his will
> For one restraint, lords of the World besides.
>
> (I, 29-32)

Milton might have sermonised in both of these instances, but he doesn't. Even before meeting Adam and Eve we are powerfully moved to pity for them. We are close to feeling, indeed, that they and Satan are in something of the same boat. Though in widely different circumstances, they have both committed the intellectual error of misunderstanding God's purposes, and are to be made to pay grievously for it.

For the moment, the relation of Adam and Eve's fall (which in *Paradise Lost* will differ in most interesting detail from that related in Genesis) has to wait. Satan has centre stage. It is impossible not to admire the rhetoric with which he tries to sustain his and his lieutenant's spirits at this juncture:

> Yet not for those,
> Nor what the potent Victor in his rage
> Can else inflict, do I repent, or change,
> Though changed in outward lustre, that fixed mind,
> And high disdain from sense of injured merit,
> That with the Mightiest raised me to contend.
>
> (I, 94-9)

There is an obduracy and intellectual haughtiness here that might even be the younger Milton speaking. And it sweeps the infernal leader on to his magnificent, brazen conclusion:

> Since through experience of this great event,
> In arms not worse, in foresight much advanced,
> We may with more successful hope resolve
> To wage by force or guile eternal war,
> Irreconcilable to our grand Foe,
> Who now triumphs, and in th' excess of joy
> Sole reigning holds the tyranny of Heaven.
>
> (I, 118-24)

It could be argued – and frequently is – that of course Satan is guilty of either intellectual failure or sheer speciousness here. He knows God is omnipotent; he and his followers have been soundly beaten, and that is that. Anna Beer (*Milton: Poet, Pamphleteer and Patriot*) points out: "Satan can't even raise his head unless God lets him do so; Satan's malice 'served but to bring forth/Infinite goodness, grace and mercy' towards man." But is this the feeling that Satan's rhetoric actually produces in us? The quotation she uses here (I, 217-18) is part of a longer authorial commentary on Satan's escape from the "fiery gulf" into which God has cast him:

> the Arch-fiend lay,
> Chained on the burning lake; nor ever thence
> Had risen, or heaved his head, but that the will
> And high permission of all-ruling Heaven
> Left him at large to his own dark designs,

> That with reiterated crimes he might
> Heap on himself damnation, while he sought
> Evil to others, and enraged might see
> How all his malice served but to bring forth
> Infinite goodness, grace, and mercy, shewn
> On Man.
>
> (I, 209-19)

It is an early example of one of Milton the moralist's periodic attempts to put a brake on the alarming proceedings his poetry has unleashed, and damp down the subversive feelings of admiration that Satan is in danger of producing in us. It introduces, somewhat precipitately, the doctrine of the "Fortunate Fall" (i.e. the idea that the Fall was a beneficial necessity, enabling God to demonstrate his infinite mercy to Man through the sacrifice of the Son) before we are anywhere near being ready for it. It is one thing for Adam at the end of the story in Book XII to be assured by the Archangel Michael that 'things aren't really so bad', when he and we have lived through the harrowing events of Eve's seduction by the Serpent, his and her reprieve from a threatened death, and the near breakdown of their hugely symbolic relationship of love. It is quite another for Milton to try to tell us after only 200-odd lines of a 10,000-word epic: 'Don't worry about any of this; at the end of the day Christ's Crucifixion and Resurrection will clear up all this mess, and Satan will be put back in his box where he belongs.' Milton the poet is already in serious conflict with Milton the theologian here – and in the battle for our sympathies the poet is winning hands down.

Moreover, is not the last line of Satan's speech, with its assertion that a victorious God "sole reigning holds the tyranny of Heaven", considerably more than mere rhetoric? Heaven, as we shall see when we go there, is certainly no parliamentary democracy. Satan here puts his finger on an uncomfortable truth about the regime which becomes an increasing difficulty for Milton as his epic unfolds. As we are to learn in Book V, it was God's appointment (or in Satan's view sudden and arbitrary imposition) of the Son as king and ruler over all Heaven's denizens that had sparked the revolt in the first place.

Satan now rallies his shattered forces. The frequent objections to Milton's uneasy mixture of spiritual being and physical sensation (which later make Raphael's attempt to explain to Adam angelic digestion and sexual activity comically incongruous) do not trouble us here. The ranks of the rebel angels are presented to us with all the solidity of a Roman legion, complete with arms, armour and ensigns. But there is an unforced poignancy in the mental effort with which they attempt to extract

> some glimpse of joy to have found their Chief
> Not in despair, to have found themselves not lost
> In loss itself;
>
> (I, 524-6)

and in their physical discomfort as they try at the same time to ignore "Their painful steps o'er the burnt soil" (I, 562). The episode calls forth some of Milton's most magnificent poetry. Satan, the warrior chief, stands before us, an image of indelible vividness:

> His form had yet not lost
> All her original brightness, nor appeared
> Less than Archangel ruined, and th' excess
> Of glory obscured: as when the sun new-risen
> Looks through the horizontal misty air
> Shorn of his beams, or, from behind the moon,
> In dim eclipse, disastrous twilight sheds
> On half the nations, and with fear of change
> Perplexes monarchs. Darkened so, yet shone
> Above them all th' Archangel: but his face
> Deep scars of thunder had intrenched, and care
> Sat on his faded cheek.
>
> (I, 591-602)

Any idea that Milton somehow *had* to write this to give God's adversary some plausibility seems immediately absurd. It is wrenched from him. Yes, the simile of the solar eclipse is the 'learned' Milton speaking, conscious of his status as an epic poet from whom such demonstrations of virtuosity (and scientific knowledge) are expected. The rest is unvarnished reality from one who had lived through times of cataclysm which gave those caught up in them no quarter. Milton was familiar with many a rise to power under arbitrary favour, and had seen equally precipitate falls from that state on a whim or from the cowardice of the original benefactor. As a political propagandist he doubtless had no reserves of sympathy. Not so as a poet. Satan, magnificent in defeat, is brought up effortlessly from the depths of his experience. And this sympathy powerfully embraces his followers,

> condemned
> For ever now to have their lot in pain –
> Millions of Spirits for his fault amerced [i.e. punished by being deprived]
> Of Heaven, and from eternal splendours flung
> For his revolt – yet faithful how they stood,
>
> (I, 607-11)

still doggedly loyal to their chief even in the depths of utter ruin and unending damnation.

It might so easily have been a fatal undertaking to try to get closer to any of these participants in the drama and imbue them with human characteristics. *Comus*, with its somewhat inert set speeches (except, tellingly, those delivered by its eponymous and 'evil' protagonist) had suggested that Milton had no natural gift for dramatic dialogue. And T.S. Eliot was famously to damn him for a generation by dismissing his "celestial and infernal regions" as "large but insufficiently furnished apartments filled by heavy talk" (essay, 'William Blake', 1920). Yet in the infernal debate in Pandemonium on the prospects that lie ahead, and the tactics to be devised to meet them, the contributing speakers effortlessly inhabit distinctive personalities. The discussion is a vibrant affair. Moloch, "the strongest and the fiercest Spirit/That fought in Heaven" (II, 44-5) comes over as Milton's equivalent of the mythological Greek hero Ajax, a man whose instinctive resort is to brute force unregulated by thought. He is "for open war. Of wiles,/More unexpert, I boast not" (II, 51-2).

Notwithstanding the catastrophic defeat that has been sustained, he has no notion of anything less than a frontal assault as a solution to the present plight:

> let us rather choose,
> Armed with Hell-flames and fury, all at once
> O'er Heaven's high towers to force resistless way,
> Turning our tortures into horrid arms
> Against the Torturer.
>
> (II, 60-4)

Naturally this is not what Satan, cannily acting as chairman of the debate, with his placeman Beëlzebub ready to intervene at the opportune moment, wants to hear. Next up, Belial, described by contrast with Moloch as "in act more graceful and humane./A fairer person lost not Heaven" (II, 109-10), recoils from the manifest folly of the suggestion and its almost inevitable consequence of extinction at the hands of God. His appeal to reason,

> To be no more. Sad cure! for who would lose,
> Though full of pain, this intellectual being,
> Those thoughts that wander through eternity,
> To perish rather, swallowed up and lost
> In the wide womb of uncreated Night,
> Devoid of sense and motion?
>
> (II, 146-51)

is a powerfully imaginative one, evoking as it does that intensely 17th century terror of what, if anything, may await us when we die. It irresistibly recalls the lines Shakespeare gives to the condemned Claudio in *Measure for Measure*, as he awaits execution in his prison cell:

> Ay, but to die and go we know not where;
> To lie in cold obstruction and to rot;
> This sensible warm motion to become
> A kneaded clod.
>
> (Act III, scene 1, 118-21)

Belial's appeal confronts the awfulness of no longer having existence as a sentient being. Milton succeeds in attributing to the fears of supposedly immortal beings the quality of our own, without there seeming anything at all incongruous about it. And having created this undeniably persuasive advocate of compromise, it seems less than just of him to editorialise at the close of Belial's speech:

> Thus Belial, with words clothed in reason's garb,
> Counselled ignoble ease and peaceful sloth.
>
> (II, 226-7)

What Belial has been advocating is hardly "peaceful sloth" – nothing about existence in Hell is ever going to be that – but merely some sort of tolerable *modus vivendi* with Heaven, to mitigate the sheer pain of their existence.

This possibility, even if it should ultimately involve a readmission to angelic service (not something Belial has actually suggested), is brusquely dismissed by Mammon. Tellingly, his vivid reminder of what such a readmission would involve, poses for the first time the question of what satisfaction is actually to be had from the angelic duties they once performed:

> Suppose he should relent
> And publish grace to all, on promise made
> Of new subjection; with what eyes could we
> Stand in his presence humble, and receive
> Strict laws imposed, to celebrate his throne
> With warbled hymns, and to his Godhead sing
> Forced hallelujahs?
>
> (II, 237-43)

The question levels a charge that never quite seems to go away in *Paradise Lost*. Without Satan to fight against, or Adam and Eve to keep watch over (a task they are conspicuously unsuccessful in), what is it that angels actually *do*? Whatever it is, we are left in no doubt that the rebel angels found it extremely irksome. "Warbled hymns" and "forced hallelujahs" hardly seem to constitute an eternity's employment for adults.

The question surfaces again in Book IV when Satan, detected in his first attempt to corrupt Eve, sneers to the archangel Gabriel that instead of going around annoying people like him, he and his squadron's

> easier business were to serve their Lord
> High up in Heaven, with songs to hymn his throne,
> And practised distances to cringe [i.e. rehearsing attitudes of obeisance],
> not fight.
>
> (IV, 943-5)

It is a sly dig from Satan who knows that he and his men gave the angels a good run for their money before God played his trump card and called up the Messiah to throw them out of Heaven. Gabriel appears stumped for an answer. Mammon's solution to the rebels' plight is not actually so different from that of Belial – minus any expectation that there may be some remission in the sentence for good behaviour. The gist is that it makes sense to remain where we are; gradually the pain will ease; there is plenty of room in the cosmos for us to live our lives down here out of God's way; the place is rich in raw materials from which we can make ourselves comfortable and create an 'alternative' empire for ourselves.

This is what the rebel angels, and Satan, want to hear (though for different reasons), and it receives an enthusiastic round of applause. They don't really want to endure again the pasting they have received. It gives Satan an opportunity to launch his surprise plan. He has already touched on a rumour that God intended to create an alternative world to Heaven, and has suggested a reconnaissance sortie to try to discover it. Beëlzebub gets to his feet to flesh out an ambitious scheme for getting back at God. It is of course Satan's, but there are psychological advantages, when addressing a gathering, in not appearing to have all the initiatives emanating from the same head.

Yet Milton does not treat Beëlzebub as a political trickster. Like Satan he is described in terms of profound respect:

> with grave
> Aspect he rose, and in his rising seemed
> A pillar of state. Deep on his front engraven
> Deliberation sat, and public care;
> And princely counsel in his face yet shone,
> Majestic, though in ruin.
>
> (II, 300-5)

There is no hint of irony here. Like his boss, Beëlzebub is a massive figure, and Milton makes no attempt to diminish him.

Beëlzebub's summing up of the 'position to date', as it were, is the masterly one of an experienced staff officer. Mere adherence to the status quo is not a realistic option. God will never allow the comfortable solution propounded by Mammon, the creation of an alternative, infernal empire. But God does have a weak spot – Man, his own latest project, newly created and placed in some "happy seat". So let us reconnoitre this place and either "possess/All as our own, and drive, as we were driven,/The puny habitants" (I, 365-7) or, even better and a much richer revenge,

> Seduce them to our party, that their God
> May prove their foe, and with repenting hand
> Abolish his own works. This would surpass
> Common revenge, and interrupt his joy
> In our confusion and our joy upraise.
>
> (II, 368-72)

This plan is approved by the infernal council: "joy/Sparkled in all their eyes: with full assent/They vote" (II, 387-9). It is a nice touch that when they have done so Beëlzebub, as some Speaker of the House of Commons might well do at the end of an emergency debate in the chamber, congratulates them on the quality of their deliberations. There *is* a democratic process here, and one feels that Milton can hardly be unaware that it contrasts markedly with the arbitrary, and often ill-tempered, decision-making processes by which Heaven is governed.

Beëlzebub resumes the podium, and the stage is set for a final decision from the "Stygian council". He calls for volunteers. Who shall undertake the perilous mission of finding out where this seat of Man is? He so eloquently impresses his audience with the perils of the journey that when he sits down

> None among the choice and prime
> Of those Heaven-warring champions could be found
> So hardy as to proffer or accept,
> Alone, the dreadful voyage.
>
> (II, 423-6)

It is Satan's opportunity to seize the leadership of the mission. But the offer has been thrown open to the floor first, and it seems unreasonable of Milton to try to guide our sympathies at the end of his acceptance speech, so as to imply that there is some chicanery on his part:

> Thus saying, rose
> The Monarch, and prevented all reply;
> Prudent lest, from his resolution raised,
> Others among the chief might offer now,
> Certain to be refused.
>
> (II, 466-70)

As Milton has already quite clearly stated, none of the others among the "millions of spirits" gathered in Pandemonium has the slightest intention of usurping Satan's privilege here. By staying in their seats they have effectively voted for him unanimously.

This is the end of Satan's 'hands-on' career as leader in *Paradise Lost*, though we are, later, taken back in time to witness him fomenting revolt and then fighting the war in Heaven. These events are interpolated in the chronology of the poem in Books V and VI, as part of Raphael's relation to Adam of the beginnings of things.

That apart, from the end of the council in Book II we shall see Satan, now as intrepid explorer, spy, sometimes tortured soul, cormorant, toad and finally as the Serpent of Genesis. Is this Satan the same being as the one Milton is still describing to us, as he prepares to leave Pandemonium flanked by his infernal peers, in such majestic terms as "their mighty Paramount …/Alone th' antagonist of Heaven, nor less/Than Hell's dread Emperor" (II, 508-10)? It's a moot point. And if the answer is that he is not, but has gradually become a diminished figure who no longer commands our respect, is this a process that has taken place organically within the poem, or is it something that has had to be imposed upon him by his creator?

Satan for the moment has exited the stage. Hereafter his rebel angels will cease to be part of the main thread of the epic's drama. Yet before we take leave of them, Milton turns aside and considers their plight with poignant sympathy. The excitement of the council and the acclaim with which they have just seen their leader off on his mission is suddenly dissipated. The powerful sense of anticlimax is beautifully observed by Milton:

> the ranged Powers
> Disband; and, wandering, each his several way
> Pursues, as inclination or sad choice
> Leads him perplexed, where he may likeliest find
> Truce to his restless thoughts, and entertain
> The irksome hours, till his great Chief return.
>
> (II, 522-7)

As we have already seen, some of the fallen angels are not among nature's thinkers, and mental peace is the last thing on their mind. We imagine Moloch is foremost among those who set out to occupy these empty hours in athletic games or warlike pursuits, fighting again amongst each other those battles in which they were not successful in the war against Heaven. These "fronted brigades form:/As when, to warn proud cities, war appears/Waged in the troubled sky" (II, 532-4).

But they are by no means all philistines. Some of them, musicians, "more mild,/Retreated in a silent valley, sing/With notes angelical" (II, 546-8) of their losses. Others

> apart sat on a hill retired,
> In thoughts more elevate, and reasoned high
> Of Providence, Foreknowledge, Will, and Fate –
> Fixed fate, free will, foreknowledge absolute,
> And found no end, in wandering mazes lost.
> Of good and evil much they argued then,
> Of happiness and final misery.
>
> (II, 557-63)

These are clearly philosophical beings. Whatever their faults we can't help feeling sorry for them in their difficulties at this juncture. They sound like educated, likeable individuals. Milton himself would undoubtedly have enjoyed their company. Certainly they are not portrayed as beings beyond redemption. In so many points at which we touch it, the infernal world seems to be a place where rational thought is applied to what we might broadly call metaphysical questions in a way that, as we shall see, is so often difficult to detect in the councils of Heaven. Apart from anything else, this Hell to which the rebel angels have been condemned is made suddenly to seem, with its silent valleys and remote hills, a not unattractive piece of countryside. While his followers try to divert themselves, Satan is embarked on his mission to try to reach the human world. With Satan the lone, intrepid explorer, as he now becomes, Milton is momentarily on less sure poetic ground than he was with Satan, leader of millions. Satan was in many ways the sum of his followers, occupying the summit of the pyramid of their combined force and aspirations. Milton could vividly embody his leadership of them in terms of grand detail. As a one-man expedition battling his way through difficult terrain, the Arch-Fiend makes a less satisfying impression. Granted there is a vigour in the poetry of

> so eagerly the Fiend
> O'er bog or steep, through strait, rough, dense, or rare,
> With head, hands, wings, or feet, pursues his way,
> And swims, or sinks, or wades, or creeps, or flies
>
> (II, 947-50)

– and Milton has been praised for his ability to step down off the heights of his grand style and deal in homely yet effective concrete detail of this kind. But there is incongruity. This does not operate on our minds as vividly as did the massive figure who levered himself ponderously from the surface of the burning lake in Book I. Satan has been cut down to size – our size. We cannot see beyond a merely dogged but muddy figure, coping as best he can with adverse circumstances on a difficult hike undertaken on a day of probably inclement weather.

An artistic excrescence that Milton might well have jettisoned is Satan's encounter with Sin (who is, it transpires, his own daughter, who had apparently sprung from his head in Heaven during the meeting of the conspirators against God) and Death (his son from a sexual encounter with this daughter that seems to have taken place not long after that). It presents us with a clutter of extraneous relationships that Milton cannot fit into his epic scheme with any conviction. And it draws him into his only excursion into allegory in *Paradise Lost*.

Sin and Death are so entirely embodied in the person of Satan that they have no real function as separate entities here. And the battle that threatens to break out between Death and Satan at their first encounter has no discernible meaning either in terms of allegory or in any literal sense. Having been seduced by Satan, Sin, as she tells him, was next raped by her son who

> in embraces forcible and foul
> Engendering with me, of that rape begot
> These yelling monsters, that with ceaseless cry
> Surround me, as thou saw'st – hourly conceived
> And hourly born, with sorrow infinite
> To me; for, when they list, into the womb
> That bred them they return, and howl, and gnaw
> My bowels, their repast.
>
> (II, 793-800)

This gruesome episode is too entirely derivative in its detail of Spenser's female monster Errour, whom we encounter in the first Canto of *The Faerie Queene*, for us not to be thoroughly thankful that Milton did not persist with the allegorical component. His imagination was not really working at this point. Sin and Death do not reappear in *Paradise Lost* until after the Fall. By that time their, somewhat obvious, significance has been subsumed in events.

These episodes apart, we first see Satan in his 'post-leadership' role in the early part of Book IV. Something has happened to the imposing figure of Books I and II. He appears to have had a psychology created for him, has become more akin to the 'human' Hamlet than to the 'archetype' Lear. The speech which begins "O thou, that, with surpassing glory crowned" (IV, 32) was, as we have already seen, thought to have been originally composed for a tragedy Milton had in mind. This Satan, a being of far greater introspection than he exhibited in Book I, delivers it, Milton tells us, overcome with sighs. It is still wonderful poetry, but it is, if you like, Euripides rather than Aeschylus, emotional rather than colossal. It is shot through with remorse, a quality quite absent from the earlier Satan's mental deliberations.

It is addressed to the sun, whose beams, Satan confesses,

> bring to my remembrance from what state
> I fell, how glorious once above thy sphere;
> Till pride and worse ambition threw me down
> Warring in Heaven against Heaven's matchless King:
> Ah, wherefore! he deserved no such return
> From me, whom he created what I was
> In that bright eminence, and with his good
> Upbraided none; nor was his service hard.
>
> (IV, 38-45)

Can this be the same Satan, we ask ourselves who, as he plotted revolt sneered at the very thought of God's service as "Knee-tribute yet unpaid, prostration vile!" (V, 782) and after the failure of his rebellion declared to his battered and bruised followers with magnificent obduracy:

> That glory never shall his wrath or might
> Extort from me. To bow and sue for grace
> With suppliant knee, and deify his power
> Who, from the terror of this arm, so late
> Doubted his empire.
>
> (I, 110-14)

It seems not. Satan at the head of his troops was not given to introspection, much less self doubt. Now, alone and pondering the consequences of his actions, he indulges in a bout of uncharacteristic mental self-flagellation. God, after all, was kind. Serving him made no unreasonable demands. Satan is guilty of base ingratitude. And, more important, Hell is not, as he thought it was, a penal sentence imposed on him by a higher power for his presumption in challenging divine authority. It is beginning to assume the character of a psychological condition, "Which way I fly is Hell; myself am Hell" (IV, 75), which afflicts him as a consequence of his setting himself against reason and order.

Is this self-abasement convincing? Does it flow naturally from the psychological movement of the narrative? Or is Milton 'cheating' here, using his authorial privilege to impose a character on Satan that is palpably at odds with the one he has so convincingly created, purely as a means of bringing that character back under control?

Critics are divided on the point. For Anna Beer this moment is consistent with what we have seen of Satan "still tormented and eloquent about his torment ... these moments of self-awareness culminate in Satan using his own glib rhetoric upon himself: 'Farewell, remorse: all good to me is lost;/Evil, be thou my good.' " (IV, 109-10). It is a perception which C.S. Lewis was broadly addressing when he stigmatised Satan's defiant assertion "Better to reign in Hell than serve in Heaven" (I, 263) as approaching "roaring farce".

Both these critics are of the 'Christian' school. By this I don't mean that as critics they are misled or governed by Christian belief in their analysis, but that they are both satisfied that Milton does succeed, as a poet, in conveying with consistency his Christian 'message' during the course of *Paradise Lost*.

It does not of course matter in the slightest whether or not we bring a Christian belief to *Paradise Lost* – none of us believes in the Olympian system that governs the *Iliad*, for example, but we take its mythology at face value. As it happens, Lewis avows his Christianity as a critic, Beer does not. But her remarks (see below in Chapter 8) on Satan and the sin of the reader suggest that she would not widely dissent from Lewis' view that "To admire Satan, then, is to give one's vote not only for a world of misery, but also for a world of lies and propaganda."

The position Lewis and Beer adopt on this question has been confronted over the years by the alternative conviction that, as William Empson (*Milton's God*) puts it, "there is a gradual calculated degradation of Satan" by Milton. (A.J.A. Waldock had used 'Satan and the Technique of Degradation' as the chapter-heading of his discussion of the Arch-Fiend's fortunes in his *Paradise Lost and its Critics*.) This is a persuasive argument, and Milton does seem to exert a consistent control over the process, maintaining it even in the flashback that the telling of the Satan story involves him in. Having been, as it were, 'cut down to size' in Book IV, where in addition to succumbing to self-doubt he is made to succumb to humiliating sexual jealousy as he watches, in the guise of a cormorant perched on the Tree of Life, Adam and Eve's love-making, Satan is portrayed as very much on his old form in Books V and VI, which recapitulate for Adam and Eve's benefit his leadership of the revolt and the war in Heaven.

The narrative is Raphael's but the tone is unmistakably Satan's. Lucifer has summoned his forces to his domain in the "north" of heaven (an imposition of the rule of the compass on the layout of heaven that doesn't somehow trouble us; Isaiah 14:13 mentions it). The declared aim is, ostensibly

> only to consult how we may best,
> With what may be devised of honours new,
> Receive him coming to receive from us
> Knee-tribute yet unpaid, prostration vile!
>
> (V, 779-82)

Satan's impetuous velocity of thought once he is set on a course of action is beautifully caught here. Before he has even got to the end of his opening proposition – which was intended, apparently, merely to outline a wholesome plan for welcoming the newly elevated Son – he has not only betrayed his resentment, but added to that the powerful insinuation that the process will in fact degrade them all. It's a resentment, we might add, that seems to be wholeheartedly shared by his audience. When Satan makes his appeal:

> Will ye submit your necks, and choose to bend
> The supple knee? Ye will not, if I trust
> To know ye right, or if ye know yourselves
> Natives and sons of Heaven possessed before
> By none; and if not equal all, yet free
>
> (V, 787-91)

it is in characteristically persuasive terms. For Satan the preservation of liberty and self-respect are at issue here.

Abdiel is the sole dissenter from it. Interestingly, he immediately denounces Satan as "Ingrate" (V, 811), a terminology exactly paralleling that of God's denunciation of Man at III, 97. The epithet does appear to be an instinctive resort of the celestial mind when it suspects disagreement with its edicts.

In the war of words that follows between Satan and Abdiel the latter seems to be considerably better primed on the facts of the creation of the angels than Satan. But there is something long-winded about Abdiel's righteousness that compares unfavourably with Satan's pithy malice. And in spite of his attempt to give the impression that there is somehow an egalitarian spirit at the heart of the celestial arrangements as they concern the Son, now appointed to rule over them all, "since he the head/One of our number thus reduced becomes" (V, 842-3), he cannot actually in the end dispel an overarching sense of arbitrary high-handedness.

The terms in which he beats his dignified retreat back to the safety of God's camp are significant:

> Yet not for thy advice or threats I fly
> These wicked tents devoted, lest the wrath
> Impendent, raging into sudden flame,
> Distinguish not.
>
> (V, 889-92)

Are we to understand that there is a distinct possibility that when God lets fly with his thunderbolts, he may not take pains to distinguish between the wicked and the righteous? Abdiel is certainly not going to hang about to risk becoming a victim of collateral bomb damage.

Yes, in the ultimate analysis, Satan is clearly intellectually in the 'wrong' in taking on an almighty power. Yet both here, and in the heat of the war in Heaven, which he manages to keep going over three days, we can't help having a sneaking regard for his bravery. At no time in all that mayhem do any of his subordinates reproach him for their sufferings. Satan never fails the test of leadership; he is consistently able to draw opinion after him.

Book IX is the dramatic heart of *Paradise Lost*. In it we return to the tormented, self doubting Satan of Book IV. As he considers the Creation that he is about to ruin he lacerates himself with the details of its variety and beauty:

> With what delight could I have walked thee round,
> If I could joy in aught, sweet interchange
> Of hill, and valley, rivers, woods, and plains,
> Now land, now sea and shores with forest crowned,
> Rocks, dens, and caves!
>
> (IX, 114-18)

The Satan who exulted in the fearful consequences of defiance has become a forlorn exile from pleasures that, he now admits, he might actually have been capable of savouring. The contemplation of the damage he is about to do no longer holds any pleasure for him. As he and Beëlzebub made the effort to drag themselves off the burning lake at the beginning of *Paradise Lost* he was able, even in the depths of pain, to brace up his lieutenant with a certain relish in the prospect of a fresh and invigorating manifesto that their new situation opened up to them: "To do aught good never will be our task/But ever to do ill our sole delight" (I, 159-60). That delight in doing ill has deserted him now. It has become something else, almost a form of neurosis. "For only in destroying I find ease/To my relentless thoughts" (IX, 129-30)

And the final humiliation galls him as he contemplates the search for the serpent who must be the instrument of his project of temptation:

> thus wrapt in mist
> Of midnight vapour glide obscure, and pry
> In every bush and brake, where hap may find
> The serpent sleeping; in whose mazy folds
> To hide me, and the dark intent I bring.
> O foul descent! that I, who erst contended
> With Gods to sit the highest, am now constrained
> Into a beast; and, mixed with bestial slime,
> This essence to incarnate and imbrute.
>
> (IX, 158-66)

Satan, who commanded armies of angels will be reduced to poking about under the shrubbery in the corners of Eden to look for the resident snake to hide in. And when the deed is done, and Eve has been induced to taste the forbidden fruit, he simply skulks away. "Back to the thicket slunk/The guilty Serpent" (IX, 784-5) . It is an astonishing come-down for "Hell's dread emperor" who left Pandemonium to such acclaim in Book II. In a morning he has undone God's work of six days and heaven knows how many more of planning, and seriously compromised the entire cosmos to boot. But Milton writes him out of the scene of his triumph in eight words.

Is Milton actually ascribing feelings of guilt to Satan here, in the conjunction of "slunk" and "guilty"? Satan has certainly had his moments of weakness in the presence of Adam and Eve. In Book IV he had seemed to allow a moment of pity to slip past his guard: "Ah! gentle pair, ye little think how nigh/Your change approaches" (IV, 366-7). And as he approached Eve on that fateful morning her grace and beauty had rendered him momentarily "Stupidly good; of enmity disarmed" (IX, 465). That likewise was an emotion from which he recovered, though not without a struggle. Perhaps Milton, who when himself contemplating Eve sometimes appears to be in thrall to his own creation, merely means us to think that in the moment when he saw that his plot against her had been successful, Satan retained some residual memory of his previous feelings for her, and could not bear to look her in the face.

It is not an emotion that survives his return to the hall of Pandemonium to make his report to his accomplices on the success of his mission. His account of Man's fall is delivered in a vein of shallow boasting that is a far cry from the dignity with which he stirred up revolt in Book V and then rallied his troops after it in Book I:

> Him by fraud I have seduced
> From his Creator; and, the more to increase
> Your wonder, with an apple; he, thereat
> Offended, worth your laughter! hath given up
> Both his beloved Man, and all his world,
> To Sin and Death a prey, and so to us.
>
> (X, 485-90)

There is something of the 'cheap shot' here. Put like this, the Fall is indeed laughable. I suppose we are entitled to say that in describing something so momentous in terms of mere fraud with an apple Satan is at least guilty of bad taste. Milton at any rate seems to have run out of the imaginative resources with which to find a suitable solution to the problem of what to do with God's great Adversary at this juncture. Satan waits for the infernal plaudits. Instead, in what is perhaps the least satisfactory single episode in *Paradise Lost,* Milton subjects him to the following humiliation:

> So having said, a while he stood, expecting
> Their universal shout, and high applause,
> To fill his ear; when, contrary, he hears
> On all sides, from innumerable tongues,
> A dismal universal hiss, the sound
> Of public scorn; he wondered, but not long
> Had leisure, wondering at himself now more,
> His visage drawn he felt to sharp and spare;
> His arms clung to his ribs; his legs entwining
> Each other, till supplanted down he fell
> A monstrous serpent on his belly prone,
> Reluctant, but in vain; a greater power
> Now ruled him, punished in the shape he sinned,
> According to his doom: he would have spoke,
> But hiss for hiss returned with forked tongue
> To forked tongue; for now were all transformed
> Alike, to serpents all.
>
> (X, 504-20)

This cannot possibly satisfy the exacting criteria for imagery that Milton has set himself in *Paradise Lost.* The fall of the rebel angels was magnificent, entrenching itself in the mind as solidly as any pictorial equivalent of it by Bruegel (who actually manages to accomplish the metamorphosis from angels to monsters without making it risible) or Rubens. This account cannot do anything similar for us. That Milton had so far to comply with Genesis that he must at some point have his Satan accomplishing the temptation of Eve by inhabiting the body of the serpent, we accept. The "dread commander" turned into a hissing snake along with his men is something that defeats the visual imagination and makes us instinctively revolt from it. We know Satan is bad, but he has deserved better than this.

Is this just a great imagination wearying as it begins to near the end of this ambitious project? Is it Milton desperately resorting to this degradation of Satan to make it clear to us that Satan's victory in Eden has actually produced a resounding defeat for him in the longer term? Or is it a symptom of something more fundamental – a subconscious recoil by Milton from a project, the defeat of a 'parliamentary' Hell by an autocratic Heaven, that he can now only achieve by what are, by his own standards, crude means?

An answer could doubtless be found in any or all of these possibilities. In any event the result is starkly unsatisfactory. Milton has his moments of what we might call visual unease in *Paradise Lost*: at points in the war in Heaven; in the discussions on the digestive systems and sex lives of angels. But here he comprehensively lets himself down in this descent to sheer melodrama.

3

The Ethos of Heaven

What is it about Milton's Heaven that is so difficult to like? It was of course never going to be easy for him to make an omniscient and omnipotent deity particularly attractive. But we might at least have expected him to have endowed a god of mercy with a faculty of sympathy for the failings of lesser beings. And on his first appearance, in Book III, Milton's God is spectacularly defective in that respect.

We first encounter him "High thron'd above all highth", surrounded by his angels who "from his sight receiv'd/Beatitude past utterance" (III, 58 and 61-2). As God looks down, the sight of the innocent Adam and Eve in Paradise gives him pleasure – but not for long. Also in view is Satan, winging his way upwards from the abyss, bent on mischief. God draws this to the attention of the Son, who is sitting at his right hand.

It's worthy of note that in his theological system (which is set out at length in *De Doctrina*) Milton tended towards Arianism. Arius (c. AD 256-336) was an Alexandrian Christian who denied the equal status of the three persons of the Trinity – and their eternal co-existence. Most controversially, the Son is not to be thought of as being 'of one substance with the Father' but as merely of 'like nature' with him, actually a subordinate being in the celestial scheme of things. Furthermore, according to Arius (who was at various times regarded by contemporaries as a heretic) there had been a time before the Son existed. Thus, Milton has the Son actually being born during the course of *Paradise Lost*. In Book V God declares to the angels:

> This day I have begot whom I declare
> My only Son,
>
> (V, 603-4)

and appoints him his deputy in the chain of command. The implication of this is that the creation of the Son therefore took place after that of the angels (though this is contradicted by what the virtuous angel Abdiel says when he tries to argue Satan out of his revolt, at V, 836ff.). In any event, it is as a subordinate, not an equal, that God now addresses the Son as he observes Satan's approach:

> Only begotten Son, seest thou what rage
> Transports our Adversary? whom no bounds
> Prescrib'd, no bars of Hell, nor all the chains
> Heap'd on him there, nor yet the main abyss
> Wide interrupt, can hold.
>
> (III, 80-4)

The tone is neutral enough, although in what follows we may feel that the "rage" the Almighty ascribes to Satan (whom, significantly, even after his defeat and expulsion from heaven, he still dignifies as "our Adversary") is in fact a projection of his own mood. God here appears to attribute the escape from the abyss to Satan's own efforts – when in fact we have already been assured (I, 209ff.) that this is all God's own work as part of the grand design. Has Milton momentarily forgotten something, or are we perhaps to take this framework of God's "high permission" (I, 212) as overarching in everything that happens in *Paradise Lost*?

In any event, the tone changes abruptly as God considers the implications for his recently created world of Satan's escape:

> For man will hearken to his glozing lies,
> And easily transgress the sole command,
> Sole pledge of his obedience: so will fall
> He and his faithless progeny: Whose fault?
> Whose but his own? Ingrate, he had of me
> All he could have; I made him just and right,
> Sufficient to have stood, though free to fall.
>
> (III, 93-9)

It is a striking transformation on God's part from "Beatitude past utterance" to white-hot rage and what seems to be an instinctive contempt for his created beings. Poor Adam, wandering hand in hand with Eve down below in Eden, has no idea that his God, above, is already castigating him for lack of gratitude for being born. The charge is the more unreasonable for being untrue. Nowhere in *Paradise Lost* does Adam blame God for the misfortunes that lead to the Fall. God's defensive 'It's not my fault; I gave him free will, didn't I?' is an unbecoming response to what he knows is about to happen.

As he goes on to consider in some detail the principle of free will not only as it applies to Man, but to the angels who fell, God now backs himself into something of a corner, intellectually. Against the fallen angels he fulminates:

> Freely they stood who stood, and fell who fell.
> Not free, what proof could they have given sincere
> Of true allegiance, constant faith, or love,
> Where only what they needs must do appear'd,
> Not what they would? What praise could they receive?
> What pleasure I, from such obedience paid.
>
> (III, 102-7)

It is a somewhat wordy rant, but the meaning is clear enough. It boils down to: 'I gave them all freedom. What on earth would have been the point of an allegiance based purely on obedience?' God seems to have forgotten what he had actually said to the assembled angels when he introduced the Son to them. At that time he told them that he was also appointing the Son absolute ruler over them all, an arrangement, so he assured them, that would make them all "for ever happy". It came with the condition:

> Him who disobeys,
> Me disobeys, breaks union, and that day,
> Cast out from God and blessed vision, falls
> Into utter darkness, deep ingulfed, his place
> Ordained without redemption, without end.
>
> (V, 611-15)

If this isn't "the tyranny of Heaven" (Satan's accusation at I, 124), what is it? The price of dissent is starkly outlined to the listening angels. We can see no discernible difference between God's threat of "utter darkness …/Ordained without redemption" for disobedience to the Son, and the punishment eventually dished out to Satan for full-scale armed revolt against the entire heavenly order. As we saw in the previous chapter, God's edict was pre-eminently the catalyst for Satan's decision to hazard just that. It is a puzzle that in his self-justification to the Son, God now seems to have forgotten so recent an episode and so fundamental a statement of intention.

The Son, who though lacking the flint and steel of the Christ of the Bible has undoubted strength of character, is anxious to keep the Father's growing anger in check here. God tells him that there are in fact quite separate plans in place for the future of mankind and for that of Satan:

> Man falls deceiv'd
> By the other first: Man therefore shall find grace,
> The other none.
>
> (III, 130-2)

What is interesting here is that this doesn't actually seem to reassure the Son. Is he afraid that the Father's anger is at such white heat that he may somehow fail to be as good as his word? It certainly strikes us as odd that he is so determined to obtain clarification on the point. His palpable anxiety that God is about to do something rash is reflected in the nervous urgency of the verse:

> For should Man finally be lost, should Man,
> Thy creature late so lov'd, thy youngest son,
> Fall circumvented thus by fraud, though join'd
> With his own folly? that be from thee far,
> That far be from thee, Father, who art judge
> Of all things made, and judgest only right.
>
> (III, 150-5)

The stammered repetition, "that be from thee far,/That far be from thee, Father", points up the filial desperation. And, just in case this hasn't been persuasive enough, the Son feels obliged to finish off his plea with the stern warning to God of how it will look to critics of the divine arrangements (and who would they be but Satan?) if he really should go so far as to abolish the Creation:

> So should thy goodness and thy greatness both
> Be question'd and blasphem'd without defence.
>
> (III, 165-6)

It is strong stuff from any son to his father, but especially so from the Son to God. It also anticipates a similar thought that is later to occur to Adam as he tries to second-guess God on the consequences of his following Eve's lead and eating the apple in Book IX. God, Adam surmises,

> would be loth
> Us to abolish, lest the Adversary
> Triumph, and say; "Fickle their state whom God
> Most favours; who can please him long? Me first
> He ruined, now Mankind; whom will he next?"
> Matter of scorn, not to be given the Foe.
>
> (IX, 946-51)

It is interesting that in thinking about the possible consequences of the Fall, both the Son and Adam have recourse to an argument that sees the issue through Satan's eyes.

God now hastens to reassure his seriously discomposed offspring that all will be well, though in a speech that makes strange reading on the page:

> Man shall not quite be lost, but sav'd who will;
> Yet not of will in him, but grace *in me*
> Freely vouchsaf'd; once more *I* will renew
> His lapsed powers, though forfeit; and enthrall'd
> By sin to foul exorbitant desires;
> Upheld *by me*, yet once more he shall stand
> On even ground against his mortal foe;
> *By me* upheld, that he may know how frail
> His fallen condition is, and *to me* owe
> All his deliverance, and to none *but me*.
>
> (III, 173-82)

The italics are mine. Might we be forgiven for thinking that they indicate all the hallmarks of megalomania?

God continues to outline in starkest terms the seriousness of man's plight after a Fall that has not yet taken place:

> Man disobeying,
> Disloyal, breaks his fealty, and sins
> Against the high supremacy of Heaven,
> Affecting God-head, and, so losing all,
> To expiate his treason hath nought left,
> But to destruction sacred and devote,
> He, with his whole posterity, must die,
> Die he or justice must.
>
> (III, 203-10)

The language is nothing if not intemperate. "Affecting God-head" is a hyperbolic description of the vanity that will actually motivate Eve to eat the forbidden fruit. Adam, as we shall see, follows her lead, only so as not to lose her, and with no idea of making himself godlike in knowledge. The notion of "destruction sacred and devote" is in the same category as the repellent cruelty of the "Priestly care" described by William Blake as he observes an innocently enquiring child stripped, bound in chains and burnt to death by the Church in his scarifying lyric 'A Little Boy Lost' (*Songs of Innocence and of Experience*, 1794). What sort of 'justice' is it, we wonder, that can only be preserved if the whole human race perishes first? We feel ourselves to be in an ambience not so much of Christian heaven as of Aztec sacrificial ceremony. This is a god who seems prepared to be up to his elbows in blood to accomplish his ends.

The only possible solution to the problem of the Fall, God explains grimly, will be in "rigid satisfaction, death for death" (III, 212). If Man (i.e. the whole of mankind) is not to die, then someone among the heavenly beings must. And then comes the call for volunteers:

> "Say, heavenly Powers, where shall we find such love?
> Which of you will be mortal, to redeem
> Man's mortal crime, and just the unjust to save?
> Dwells in all Heaven charity so dear?"
> He ask'd, but all the heavenly Quire stood mute,
> And silence was in Heav'n: on man's behalf.
>
> (III, 213-18)

The angels are abashed at the enormity of what they are asked to do. None of them wants to step forward.

There are several points to be made here. First, we have already had this type of *coup de théâtre*, in Beëlzebub's appeal to the rebel angels (II, 402), and from an artistic point of view it doesn't bear repetition. This is in any case not nearly as dramatically effective as its infernal counterpart, and the lack of vitality in the verse in which God asks his (really rhetorical) question reflects that.

And after all, isn't there something simply *unseemly* about it on the most basic level? *Why* does God pull such a stunt? Why humiliate his angels when he knows – and we know – perfectly well what the solution to man's redemption will be? Tinkering with the scriptures at this juncture is not an option for Milton and there was no need to elaborate on: "For God so loved the world that he gave his only begotten Son, that whosoever believeth in him should not perish, but have everlasting life" (John 3:16) in the way he does here. There are plenty of instances in *Paradise Lost* in which Milton does improve on the biblical version of events. This is not one of them.

Nevertheless Milton presses on. Like Satan in Pandemonium, the Son steps in and saves the day:

> Behold me then: me for him, life for life,
> I offer: on me let thine anger fall;
> Account me Man; I for his sake will leave
> Thy bosom, and this glory next to thee
> Freely put off, and for him lastly die
> Well pleased; on me let Death wreak all his rage.
> Under his gloomy power I shall not long
> Lie vanquished. Thou hast given me to possess
> Life in myself for ever.
>
> (III, 236-44)

For Joseph Addison, the Messiah was the true hero of *Paradise Lost*. He was taking issue (*Spectator*, 9th February 1712) with Dryden, the first champion of Satan for that honour. Certainly with victory over the rebel angels and the redemption of Mankind against his name, the Son might seem to have all the heroic credentials. Yet, as the matter is explained to us here, there is no perceived risk. Offering himself as a sacrifice, the Son knows that he will "not long lie vanquished". Everlasting life lies just round the corner.

Strangely, the very thought seems suddenly to imbue him not with humility but with some of the savagery of temper that afflicts the Father:

> I through the ample air in triumph high
> Shall lead Hell captive maugre [i.e. in spite of] Hell, and show
> The powers of darkness bound. Thou, at the sight
> Pleased, out of Heaven shalt look down and smile,
> While, by thee raised, I ruin all my foes;
> Death last, and with his carcase glut the grave.
>
> (III, 254-9)

Milton is always at pains to stress the Son's meekness. But this deserts him here, in his account of redemption, which emphasises not peace and love for redeemed mankind, but rather the jail and charnel house for vanquished Hell and Death. God and the Son make an unattractive pair in this scene as they descant on the details of the brilliant schemes they have cooked up for the defeat of Satan and the redemption of mankind. At one point the Father tells us that "heavenly love shall outdo hellish hate" (III, 298). The idea of competition between Heaven and Hell in what should be a context of redemption and salvation is an odd notion to have to grasp.

It is always Milton's problem in relation to his manifest concern that God shall be seen as a beneficent being, that he is never in fact able to make him attractive to us either in his methods or with the outcomes they are aimed at bringing about. God displays uneasiness, verging on paranoia, towards the Creation. On the most basic level he simply doesn't *trust* anyone. He certainly never seems confident that the safety measures he has supposedly put in place can preserve the security of Eden, and is sensitive to any criticism that might be made of them.

Therefore, when he sends Raphael down to the garden to warn Adam of the dangers he faces from Satan it must be "Lest, wilfully transgressing, he pretend/Surprisal, unadmonished, unforewarned" (V, 244-5).

One of the most serious concerns for both Milton and God, here, is the somewhat dubious provenance of the Creation itself. In *Paradise Lost* it simply wasn't the first thing on God's mind. In the Old Testament we are in no doubt that the creation of the world is the beginning of the story – the beginning of everything. "In the beginning, God created the heaven and the earth" (Genesis 1:1). But it is very far from being the beginning of events as they unfold in *Paradise Lost*. The Garden of Eden and Adam and Eve, are quite explicitly created only in reaction to the depopulation of Heaven through the loss of the rebel angels. God reflects ruefully to the Son on the damage done by Satan:

> But, lest his heart exalt him in the harm
> Already done, to have dispeopled Heaven,
> My damage fondly deemed, I can repair
> That detriment, if such it be to lose
> Self-lost; and in a moment will create
> Another world, out of one man a race
> Of men innumerable, there to dwell,
> Not here; till, by degrees of merit raised,
> They open to themselves at length the way
> Up hither, under long obedience tried;
> And Earth be changed to Heaven, and Heaven to Earth,
> One kingdom, joy and union without end.
>
> (VII, 150-61)

The purposes of the Creation are made quite explicit, here. They are twofold: (a) to get back at Satan and to demonstrate to him that making off with a third of Heaven's garrison is merely "damage fondly deemed". It is clearly more than that or God would not need to resort to plan (b) which is that the creation of the earth is designed to provide a reserve of manpower which, if its members learn to behave themselves "under long obedience tried", will become spiritually fit to be admitted to heaven to make good the gaps in the angelic ranks there. In short, God *is* smarting over the revolt, as well he might be. To have a revolt against you is one thing – though if you are an all-powerful God, bad enough. To have a third of your people joining in such a revolt is surely a sign of serious mismanagement which must shake your faith in your own judgement.

And of course, even as he elaborates this scheme to the Son, God has to face the fact that his plan for the reinforcement of Heaven in this way is going to be a crashing failure even before it gets under way. Man will simply never measure up to the grandiose destiny that God has in mind for him. Satan will see to that. This is perhaps the only juncture at which we feel a sneaking sympathy for God. At this precise moment the eventual 'victory' – Christ's redemption of Man through his death on the Cross – seems too impossibly far in the future to be of immediate consolation.

Indeed the question of God's control over events, as depicted during the narrative sections of *Paradise Lost*, is an ambiguous one. With Satan drawing together his forces to challenge the elevation of the Son as head of the angelic host, God addresses his new commander-in-chief, the Son, in terms that surely fall some way short of assurance of the outcome:

> Nearly it now concerns us to be sure
> Of our Omnipotence, and with what arms
> We mean to hold what anciently we claim
> Of deity or empire: Such a foe
> Is rising, who intends to erect his throne
> Equal to ours, throughout the spacious north;
> Nor so content, hath in his thought to try
> In battle, what our power is, or our right.
> Let us advise, and to this hazard draw
> With speed what force is left, and all employ
> In our defence; lest unawares we lose
> This our high place, our sanctuary, our hill.
>
> (V, 721-32)

If words are to mean anything, surely they express real doubt here? God's concern is apparent. Divine omnipotence is going to be tested. We have a genuine contest on our hands. We have got to move fast and deploy what forces we have left to meet the coming attack. If we let ourselves be taken by surprise we shall lose everything.

In the face of this, the Son's answer is frankly puzzling:

> Mighty Father, thou thy foes
> Justly hast in derision, and, secure,
> Laughest at their vain designs.
>
> (V, 735-7)

Is this a private joke between Father and Son? God is not laughing as far as we can detect. There is nothing sarcastic in his tone. His warning appears to demand that it should be taken at face value. Milton is certainly not underplaying the threat:

> So spake the Son; but Satan, with his Powers,
> Far was advanced on winged speed; an host
> Innumerable as the stars of night.
>
> (V, 743-5)

The imagination of the poet cannot help thrilling to the sight of this rapidly advancing foe. There is an involuntary sense of awe on his part as well as ours at the well-nigh beautiful spectacle of Lucifer's starry hosts.

And isn't the planting of "but" where it is in line 743 a deliberate indication that the Son's reaction to the parental fears betrays a perilous lack of urgency? We are given the clear impression that Satan's attack, with an extremely large army, is ahead of any anticipated schedule as far as the defenders are concerned, and that this is no time for sitting around.

Milton is of course in something of a cleft stick here. The Satanic threat has to be depicted as an impressive one, to make its defeat laudable. Therefore the War in Heaven will occupy three days and the whole of Book VI. The 'bottom line' is, of course, celestial omnipotence. Nevertheless the Son's complacent assumption of it here, as commander-in-chief, sits oddly with his Father's palpable anxiety about the outcome, as head of the executive. At this moment God actually seems a marginally more sympathetic being than his Son.

Is there in fact a gradual softening of the image of God as the poem proceeds? The anger he expended in anticipating the Fall is absent from his response once it has taken place. When the angelic guards, who have been on constant patrol to try to prevent Satan's entry to Eden, return to Heaven mute and chastened in Book X, he is mildness personified:

53

> be not dismayed,
> Nor troubled at these tidings from the earth,
> Which your sincerest care could not prevent,
>
> (X, 35-7)

And from this point on he delegates to others the unpleasant necessities of the postlapsarian period. The Son is despatched down to Eden as his representative for the judgement scene of Genesis 3:8-19. He sends the Archangel Michael to drive Adam and Eve out of the Garden, giving him at the same time considerable latitude about how it is to be done. Although Michael must: "Without remorse drive out the sinful pair" (XI, 105) the earlier censoriousness seems to have dissipated, to have been replaced with a kindly resignation:

> Yet, lest they faint
> At the sad sentence rigorously urged,
> (For I behold them softened, and with tears
> Bewailing their excess), all terror hide.
> If patiently thy bidding they obey,
> Dismiss them not disconsolate; reveal
> To Adam what shall come in future days.
>
> (XI, 108-14)

Michael is not to bawl out the errant pair, the mere thought of whose faults filled God with such incandescent fury in Book III. In their penitent state they are to be gently handled, and if they are good, so to speak, they can be treated to a consoling glimpse into the future. Has God, we ask ourselves, learnt something, too, from the creation of an over-elaborate system, which required so little to derail it?

4

Adam and Eve in Eden

By the time we first encounter Adam and Eve in Book IV we are full of curiosity about what Milton will make of them. The view of them from Heaven has not been encouraging. Admittedly God was in a petulant mood, but even reading between the flashes of his anger, the protagonists of his creation were made to seem a pretty poor lot. Presenting them, now, as he does through the jealous eye of the watching Satan, Milton dispels that impression. From his vantage point on the Tree of Life where he sits in the guise of a cormorant, Satan grudgingly surveys the beauty and variety of living things, bird, beast and flower, wanting to hate everything yet not quite succeeding. Suddenly, he is confronted by

> Two of far nobler shape, erect and tall,
> Godlike erect, with native honour clad
> In naked majesty seemed lords of all:
> And worthy seemed; for in their looks divine
> The image of their glorious Maker shone.
>
> (IV, 288-92)

It is a dramatic moment, and one that sets the tone for our view of Adam and Eve. These are not naïve young lovers set in the garden to canoodle their way blindly to disaster, but creatures of maturity and majesty. Some of the most beautiful poetry to be found in *Paradise Lost* is associated with them. Yes, Milton must 'toe the party line' about the relative merits of the sexes – how could he do otherwise in the age he inhabited, and given the story he has embarked on?

> For contemplation he and valour formed;
> For softness she and sweet attractive grace;
> He for God only, she for God in him:
> His fair large front and eye sublime declared
> Absolute rule.
>
> (IV, 297-301)

The greatness of Milton is that he cannot sustain this piece of male-orientated complacency in relation to Eve as the poem progresses. She will not be categorised like this. If Adam at this introduction had no idea that the "Absolute rule" ascribed to him will go unchallenged, then perhaps he might have taken greater note of Eve's "wanton ringlets" (IV, 306). Several critics have been at pains to stress that the word "wanton" means here merely "luxuriant", "dishevelled" or "uncontrolled", that it has not at this stage of the English language's development acquired a sexual connotation too. It certainly has, as the most random reading of Shakespeare indicates. Milton would never have risked using such a word at this juncture without being aware of its implications. Unconsciously or not, he hints at a female psychology that portends some trouble for Adam. From the moment we see her, Eve stands before us brilliantly alive.

One might almost say that as his relationship with her develops, Milton himself almost becomes in thrall to her charms. For him at this moment, Adam and Eve are simply "the loveliest pair,/That ever since in love's embraces met" (IV, 321-2). God's waspish account of their frailties in Book III is banished from our minds in this unconditionally generous assessment of them.

Do Adam and Eve have sex before the Fall? It seems that they don't in the Old Testament. It is not until after their dismissal from the garden that we are told: "And Adam knew Eve his wife; and she conceived and bare Cain." (Genesis 4:1). Sex is a function of sin. The product of it, Cain, will become the world's first murderer and fratricide. There might have been a certain mileage for Milton in associating sex with the original sin of eating the Forbidden Fruit (which is what he appears to want to do in its disturbing resurgence after the Fall in Book IX). Here in Book IV, he does not immediately settle the question. There is something provisional about "nor turned, I ween,/Adam from his fair spouse, nor Eve the rites/Mysterious of connubial love refused" (IV, 741-3).

But of course she doesn't. From the very moment we see her there is no hint of maidenly modesty about Eve. She knows exactly what she has been put on earth for. God made it clear at the outset, just after he had created her from Adam's rib:

>   follow me,
> And I will bring thee where no shadow stays
> Thy coming, and thy soft embraces – he
> Whose image thou art; him thou shalt enjoy
> Inseparably thine, to him shalt bear
> Multitudes like thyself.
>
> (IV, 469-74)

This is the most wholehearted encouragement to Eve that could be envisaged. (The self-avowedly celibate God is seen at his most approachable and understanding here.) 'Enjoy' is of course the 17th-century terminology for 'have sexual intercourse with'. And with Milton, as so often in Shakespeare (Juliet, Goneril), enjoyment of that pleasure is recognised as being by no means an exclusively male prerogative. In our first glimpse of the couple, Eve has not been with Adam for five minutes it seems (the chronology of these early encounters is left deliberately vague) before she

>   half-embracing leaned
> On our first father; half her swelling breast
> Naked met his, under the flowing gold
> Of her loose tresses.
>
> (IV, 494-7)

Adam will not, we imagine, long resist this beautifully evoked assault on his susceptibilities.

It is difficult not to feel sympathy for Satan as he watches the human couple's lovemaking from his solitary perch. "Sight hateful, sight tormenting! thus these two,/Imparadised in one another's arms" (IV, 505-06). The critics on the whole have been somewhat unfeeling over Satan's reaction. Frank Kermode (in his essay 'Adam Unparadised', in *The Living Milton*) went so far as to call him "an old voyeur". But Satan doesn't have to "look through a peephole" as Kermode accuses him of doing. It is not night-time and we are not in the bedchamber. One imagines that, with absolutely no restraints on anything they did (apart from eating the Apple), Adam and Eve simply lay down and consummated their relationship on the bountiful green bosom of nature, as they saw the rest of God's creation doing.

This is all very well of course. But one cannot make love all day long. Outside that delightful activity, are Adam and Eve in danger of getting bored in Eden? They have of course their daily programme of horticulture to keep abreast of, but is that not made to seem a trifle futile? Two pairs of hands (which would rather be employed about each other) do seem quite inadequate to look after what we imagine to be a vast creation of many acres, one that is simply rioting in growth.

As Adam explains, when detailing the next day's labours to Eve, they appear to be falling behind in their work. While all the other animals can please themselves in what they do,

> To-morrow, ere fresh morning streak the east
> With first approach of light, we must be risen,
> And at our pleasant labour, to reform
> Yon flowery arbours, yonder alleys green,
> Our walk at noon, with branches overgrown,
> That mock our scant manuring, and require
> More hands than ours to lop their wanton growth.
>
> (IV, 623-9)

The human pair must be up before the crack of dawn to undertake a work schedule that in spite of Adam's description of it as "pleasant labour" is clearly causing him great anxiety. At a later date Eve will propose a division of labour that will lead to their downfall. For now, all serenity, she is in no mood to allow herself to be worried by Adam's concerns. Instead of answering them, she turns to him "with perfect beauty adorned" and delivers to his face the most beautiful love poem he will ever hear, the first love poem, if we like to think it so, in the world, and one of the most marvellous outpourings of lyrical emotion Milton ever composed:

> Sweet is the breath of Morn, her rising sweet,
> With charm of earliest birds: pleasant the sun,
> When first on this delightful land he spreads
> His orient beams, on herb, tree, fruit, and flower,
> Glistering with dew; fragrant the fertile earth
> After soft showers; and sweet the coming on

Of grateful Evening mild; then silent Night,
With this her solemn bird, and this fair moon,
And these the gems of Heaven, her starry train:
But neither breath of Morn, when she ascends
With charm of earliest birds; nor rising sun
On this delightful land; nor herb, fruit, flower,
Glistering with dew; nor fragrance after showers;
Nor grateful Evening mild; nor silent Night,
With this her solemn bird, nor walk by moon,
Or glittering star-light, without thee is sweet.

(IV, 641-56)

It is Eve's love song not only to Adam, but to the Creation itself. Its repetitions, "the breath of morn", "Glistering with dew", "silent night with this her solemn bird", impart to it the spell-binding quality of an incantation, and build up to the simple yet powerful expression of Eve's great love for Adam, which is dropped into the last half-line. If we ever find ourselves getting bored with Milton's efforts to stress the perfection of nature, this, read out loud, is the antidote.

Adam is Milton's protagonist in this drama of Eden, but Eve takes over our imagination as her husband never can. One moment the lens of Milton's eye sees her amid the fruits of Eden as some Flora of Roman wall painting as she "strows the ground/With rose and odours" (V, 348-9) in preparation for the reception of an angelic guest. The sight of her draws from Milton some of his simplest, most direct, imagery. He cannot help reminding us of her nakedness, whether she is standing modestly to receive the Archangel Raphael: "but Eve,/Undecked save with herself, more lovely fair/Than Wood-Nymph" (V, 379-81); or serving Adam and his angelic guest: "Mean while at table Eve/Ministered naked" (V, 443-4). And when he sends her, growing bored with Adam's metaphysical enquiries, out into Eden for some fresh air he seems to have completely forgotten that she is the biblical mother of mankind, whom the archangel has not long before hailed with "the holy salutation used/Long after to blest Mary, second Eve" (V, 386-7):

> With Goddess-like demeanour forth she went,
> Not unattended; for on her, as Queen,
> A pomp [i.e. procession] of winning Graces waited still,
> And from about her shot darts of desire
> Into all eyes, to wish her still in sight.
>
> (VIII, 59-63)

What *is* Milton up to, letting Eve loose on Paradise like this? She has suddenly stepped out of her biblical milieu into an erotically charged classical landscape in which she undergoes apotheosis as Aphrodite, the Greek goddess of sexual love. Heaven's watchful cherubim, who should be keeping an eye on her, have given way to the Graces, in classical mythology the three female attendants on Aphrodite. Though they actually behave more like a swarm of mischievous putti or Cupids, who, as if the sight of the naked Eve were not enough to raise the temperature among all beholders, have been given the job of firing love-darts at anyone in the vicinity. Milton creates a sensuous vision completely at odds with the worthy atmosphere of the question-and-answer session on the meaning of the universe that is being conducted near by in their Eden home between Adam and Raphael.

Up to this point Adam has seemed a somewhat static character. It is not his fault. There simply isn't enough for him to do in Eden. Yes, he has his love, but he does not habitually express himself on that subject with Eve's instinctive lyrical fluency. His love for her is also tempered by the responsibility that befits him as head of the human race. He is necessarily a conduit for God's injunctions about human conduct – such of them, that is, as he has been made privy to. Thus, almost his first words to Eve are to convey the prohibition on eating the fruit of the Tree of Knowledge. By comparison with Eve he is bound to come over as practical and prosaic.

The arrival of Raphael is a godsend. Adam now emerges as an intelligent enquirer after the truth of things, who does not like to be fobbed off with half-answers. There are a number of moments, indeed, when we wonder whether or not Raphael is drawn by Adam's questions beyond his strict remit from God, and out of his own comfort zone. Quite early on in a session between them that extends over four books we are amused to hear from Adam that he is finding some aspects of the

Edenic life a little tedious. His response to Raphael's answer to his first round of questions is interesting:

> Thy words
> Attentive, and with more delighted ear,
> Divine instructor, I have heard, than when
> Cherubic songs by night from neighbouring hills
> Aereal music send.
>
> (V, 544-8)

Is there not something verging on the insurrectionary about Adam's thanks here? His gratitude does seem a little double-edged. We might paraphrase: 'It's nice to have some rational explanation of why we're here, as an alternative to this diet of holy songs we have had up till now.' The nightly angelic muzak is clearly becoming tedious. Adam's response to it is in marked contrast with Raphael himself, who elsewhere reports with approval on an entire day "spent/In song and dance about the sacred hill" (V, 618-9). This version of the angelic function takes us uncomfortably close to Satan's gibe to Abdiel about "Ministring Spirits, trained up in feast and song!" (VI, 167) at the outset of the War in Heaven.

There comes a point where Adam's inquisition clearly begins to irritate Raphael. When he boldly comments on the structure of the visible universe,

> I oft admire,
> How Nature wise and frugal could commit
> Such disproportions, with superfluous hand
> So many nobler bodies to create
>
> (VIII, 25-8)

(i.e. 'Just what is the point of all these heavenly bodies if only heaven and earth are inhabited? It all seems such a waste'), he receives the dusty answer: "Sollicit not thy thoughts with matters hid" (VIII, 167).

But we admire his persistence. Another check awaits him in his account to Raphael of how he feels about Eve. The archangel, we feel, is not at all comfortable with this, even though Adam is at pains to assure him that his devotion to his wife is to her mental and spiritual qualities:

61

> "Greatness of mind and Nobleness their seat
> Build in her loveliest, and create an awe
> About her, as a guard angelick placed."
> To whom the Angel with contracted brow:
> "Accuse not Nature, she hath done her part;
> Do thou but thine."
>
> (VIII, 557-62)

The "contracted brow" is a nice touch. Raphael is not at ease in the role of personal-relationships counsellor. Adam is not, of course, blaming anyone for anything here, merely enthusing on the sheer delightfulness, from all points of view, of the situation in which he finds himself. At the same time he is able to express to Raphael the entirely admirable homage to Eve that he doesn't quite get round to delivering to her in person.

God may have sanctioned sex and told Eve to go and enjoy it. Raphael will have none of it:

> But if the sense of touch, whereby mankind
> Is propagated, seem such dear delight
> Beyond all other; think the same vouchsafed
> To cattle and each beast.
>
> (VIII, 579-82)

In other words: beasts propagate by "sense of touch" (i.e. sexual intercourse), so don't think there's anything so special about it. It's the one thing that makes you like them. Poor Adam. He has gone out of his way to stress Eve's qualities of mind and Raphael *will* insist that he is merely a slave to sex.

Are we to take it that Raphael's position here is to be equated with Milton's? One would have hoped not, given the unconditional paean the poet paid to her captivating loveliness in Book V. But it would surely be equally unlikely that he would bring one of God's archangels on to the stage to utter opinions with which he was at odds. We are here in the presence of another of those conflicts between Milton the moralist and Milton the poet, in which the poet's viewpoint is, as so often in *Paradise Lost*, the more attractive, and more humane.

At the end of his hostile peroration Raphael implies that the original intention was for Adam to remain mateless ("for which cause,/Among the beasts no mate for thee was found", VIII, 593-4), presumably as a mirror-image of the celibate God. This would seem to be nonsense if God intended his human race to be a means of repopulating a Heaven depleted by Satan's revolt.

Adam is "half abashed" at being told, yet again, that he is on the road to becoming "sunk in carnal pleasure" (VIII, 593). But he returns to the argument with some spirit to assure Raphael that it is Eve's mind and not her body that captivates him, in terms that do credit to both his heart and his understanding. Adam's is really the last word. His next question puts Raphael thoroughly on the back foot:

> Bear with me then, if lawful what I ask:
> Love not the heavenly Spirits, and how their love
> Express they? by looks only? or do they mix
> Irradiance, virtual or immediate touch?
>
> (VIII, 614-17)

In other words: 'Is lovemaking in Heaven real or virtual?' Poor Raphael, now. It does not help that Milton has him answering "with a smile that glowed/Celestial rosy red, Love's proper hue" (VIII, 618-19). However many times we read this we can only think of it as a blush of embarrassment on a topic on which Raphael is ill-informed. His confused and unconvincing answer does nothing to dispel that impression.

Raphael has had enough of this inquisition. Time is pressing and he must get back to Heaven. He has not by any means had the debate all his own way.

5

The Fall

The Fall is sensed long before Eve's encounter with the Serpent in Book IX. The vulnerability of the earthly couple was hinted at in Book IV when we (in the company of the Archangel Gabriel and his scouting party) encountered Satan in Eden, "Squat like a toad, close at the ear of Eve,/Assaying by his devilish art to reach/The organs of her fancy" (IV, 800-2). Confronted by Gabriel, Satan is compelled to back off.

It is not until Book V that we learn whether or not his mission has been successful. It is a scene keenly observed by Milton who presents his human pair at their most appealing as they are confronted with the first inklings of adversity. Adam awakes to a beautiful dawn, vividly alive to its birdsong, rustling leaves and tinkling streams, only "to find unwakened Eve/With tresses discomposed, and glowing cheek,/As through unquiet rest" (V, 9-11). Everything about this description rings alarm bells. Milton suggests a psychological dimension to her state of disorder in describing her hair as "discomposed". Her "glowing cheek" we immediately feel has a fevered quality and is nothing to do with sweet dreams of love.

Startled awake by his touch and whispered endearments ("My fairest, my espoused, my latest found,/Heaven's last best gift, my ever new delight!" (V, 19-20), a moving expression of sheer love), Eve relates the dream that has, unknown to her and Adam, been Satan's handiwork:

> for I this night
> (Such night till this I never passed) have dreamed,
> If dreamed, not, as I oft am wont, of thee,
> Works of day past, or morrow's next design,
> But of offence and trouble, which my mind
> Knew never till this irksome night.
>
> (V, 30-5)

The fractured, stuttering account, contained as it is in a single tumbling sentence which goes back on its thoughts, and then darts sideways into a parenthesis, effectively expresses the disordered state of mind which we suspected from the sight of her in sleep. Even before she acquaints us with the substance of the dream we feel that she has somehow become tainted.

The dream itself has two components. It is a dress rehearsal for Eve's future temptation, not in this instance by the Serpent but, as she relates to Adam, "One shaped and winged like one of those from Heaven/By us oft seen" (V, 55-6). This 'angelic' apparition leads her to the Tree of Knowledge. There, with him, she eats its fruit, and

> Forthwith up to the clouds
> With him I flew, and underneath beheld
> The earth outstretched immense, a prospect wide
> And various: wondering at my flight and change
> To this high exaltation.
>
> (V, 86-90)

Eve's second dream experience parallels the New Testament temptation of Christ, borne aloft by Satan to survey and be offered the kingdoms of the earth (Matthew 4:1-11, Luke 4:1-13) in exchange for worshipping him. Eve of course sees merely "a prospect wide/And various" since she as yet knows nothing of kingdoms or politics. In her dream Satan does not get the chance to make his offer. He is disturbed by Gabriel. But we have no great confidence, had he had the chance to do so, that she would have been able to emulate the New Testament Christ and turn his proposal down. In her dream she has already eaten the Apple without a qualm. Now, "Wondering at my flight and change/To this high exaltation", she appears rather to be elated by the experience than otherwise. "Exaltation" is, here, a deliberately charged word, doing duty both for the physical altitude to which Satan has conducted her, to show her the view, and the giddy sense of spiritual uplift she feels at being there.

Eve is thoroughly alarmed, not merely at the thought of having had a dream so far outside her experience, but by the role she has apparently willingly played in it. Adam does his best to reassure her:

> Evil into the mind of God or Man
> May come and go, so unreproved, and leave
> No spot or blame behind: which gives me hope
> That what in sleep thou didst abhor to dream,
> Waking thou never will consent to do.
>
> (V, 117-21)

This is well meant but it does not really answer the problem that is troubling Eve. The fact is that in her dream she fell once and looked like being on the way to sin a second time had not Gabriel intervened. Her dream has revealed to Eve a disturbing propensity to be curious about matters that seem to be outside God's agenda for her.

What we might call Phase Two of the Fall, begins in an atmosphere of palpably altered dynamics in the Adam/Eve relationship. The Eve of Book IX is a radically changed creature from the woman of Book IV, to whom Adam was "My Author and Disposer, what thou bidst/Unargued I obey" (IV, 635-6). Her share in the stewardship of Eden has, it would appear, imbued her with a certain self confidence. In Book VIII we saw her growing bored with the metaphysical discussion between Adam and Raphael:

> So spake our sire, and by his countenance seemed
> Entering on studious thoughts abstruse; which Eve
> Perceiving, where she sat retired in sight,
> With lowliness majestic from her seat,
> And grace that won who saw to wish her stay,
> Rose, and went forth among her fruits and flowers,
> To visit how they prospered.
>
> (VIII, 39-45)

Eve thinks that this discussion is becoming overcomplicated. She steps outside to get on with some useful gardening.

We are free to imagine that the events of Book IX, which opens on the morning of the Fall itself, take place on the day after Raphael returns to Heaven. The day begins with a spirited show of independence from Eve. Adam, momentarily lapsing into a prosing assumption of superiority of the kind he has not long before endured from Raphael, to a certain extent brings her rebelliousness on himself. In Book IV he had shared with her his worries that maintenance works in Eden were falling behind schedule. Now he finds himself, in the opening conversational exchanges of the day, hoist with his own petard. Eve proposes a division of labour as a means of increasing productivity – each going their separate ways in the Garden and meeting again at suppertime to compare notes on progress. This alarms Adam, who wants to keep an eye on her. Given his own previous concerns, her arguments are, of course, unanswerable. He is forced into backtracking, which he does in a patronising tone that is not likely to recommend itself to Eve in her present mood of self-assertion:

> nothing lovelier can be found
> In woman, than to study household good,
> And good works in her husband to promote.
> Yet not so strictly hath our Lord imposed
> Labour, as to debar us when we need
> Refreshment, whether food, or talk.
>
> (IX, 232-7)

It's quite admirable, he says, that the little woman wants to try to understand the economics of estate management so that she can help her husband, but God did say that they don't have to overdo things to the extent of having to spend time apart from each other. He then makes the fatal error of telling her that she is the weak link in the relationship:

> leave not the faithful side
> That gave thee being, still shades thee, and protects.
> The wife, where danger or dishonour lurks,
> Safest and seemliest by her husband stays.
>
> (IX, 265-8)

Everything about Adam's approach to Eve here is calculated to get her back up. The "faithful side/That gave thee being" is a tactless dig, reminding her that she was formed, after him (and, at that, only at his request) from one of his ribs. She is Wo-man to his Man (in the Hebrew Bible *Ishshah*, as having been taken out of *Ish*, the Man, deriving life from him and therefore inferior). Adam's warning over potential "dishonour"

67

introduces the implication that she is not to be trusted from a moral point of view. This is not the language this 'new Eve' is likely to tolerate – and she doesn't. As Milton makes quite clear in a beautifully – and humorously – observed passage, it is their first tiff. Eve is nettled. She replies "As one who loves, and some unkindness meets" (IX, 271), and although Milton assures us that her reaction is given in terms of "sweet austere composure", it is made quite clear as she flings his imputation back in his face that she has no intention of backing down:

> But, that thou shouldst my firmness therefore doubt
> To God or thee, because we have a foe
> May tempt it, I expected not to hear.
> His violence thou fearest not, being such
> As we, not capable of death or pain,
> Can either not receive, or can repel.
> His fraud is then thy fear; which plain infers
> Thy equal fear, that my firm faith and love
> Can by his fraud be shaken or seduced;
> Thoughts, which how found they harbour in thy breast,
> Adam, misthought of her to thee so dear?
>
> (IX, 279-89)

Eve has come a long way from her earlier, prettily expressed contentment with a submissive role in 'men's affairs'. Adam does not fear physical attack, and neither shall she. They have both been created "not capable of death or pain". His doubts on the score of her supposedly greater vulnerability must therefore centre on his fear that she can somehow be "seduced". Adam has gone too far and now gets the 'How *could* you ...?' treatment.

From this point he is always on the back foot and resorts to increasingly desperate (and wordy) arguments. Milton, whether speaking for himself or through the mouth of his characters, so often betrays his lack of conviction by becoming prolix, as Adam is here. This mental shuffling of feet is in marked contrast to Eve's sweetly trenchant directness:

> Not diffident of thee do I dissuade
> Thy absence from my sight, but to avoid
> The attempt itself, intended by our foe.
> For he who tempts, though in vain, at least asperses
> The tempted with dishonour foul; supposed
> Not incorruptible of faith, not proof
> Against temptation: Thou thyself with scorn
> And anger wouldst resent the offered wrong.
>
> (IX, 293-300)

In other words: 'It's not that I don't trust you, dear, I just don't want you to be insulted even by the attempt to tempt you. You know you'd be really angry if that happened.'

As Eve argues him into acquiescence in her demands, she begins to sound more and more like the Milton of political persuasion, an impassioned apologist for personal liberty. What on earth is the point, she says, "thus to dwell/In narrow circuit straitened by a foe/… How are we happy, still in fear of harm?" (IX, 322-6). God himself, she argues, would think the better of us if we could face down this threat ourselves. And she proceeds to her trump card: " … what is faith, love, virtue, unassayed/Alone, without exteriour help sustained?" (IX, 335-6).

Milton's Eve is by this time robustly restating the position he had set out in the celebrated passage in *Areopagitica*:

> I cannot praise a fugitive and cloistered virtue, unexercised and unbreathed, that never sallies out and sees her adversary, but slinks out of the race where that immortal garland is to be run for, not without dust and heat.

Like him, she has become a militant crusader for freedom of action based on the individual conscience. She perfectly exemplifies the clash between Milton's libertarian instincts and his necessary belief in an authoritarian God.

Adam's final resort is the unattractive schoolmasterly injunction, "Wouldst thou approve thy constancy, approve/First thy obedience" (IX, 367-8), before he gives way with scarcely disguised ill-grace:

> Go; for thy stay, not free, absents thee more;
> Go in thy native innocence, rely
> On what thou hast of virtue; summon all!
> For God towards thee hath done his part, do thine.
>
> (IX, 372-5)

It precisely echoes the injunction, "Accuse not Nature, she hath done her part;/Do thou but thine", with which Raphael tried to dampen Adam's lively enthusiasm in Book VIII. Eve is magnanimous in victory." ... I go, nor much expect/A foe so proud will first the weaker seek" (IX, 382-3). She is to be completely wrong about that of course. But it is at least gracious of her to imply that if there is to be an attempt on them by Satan, she expects it to be directed against Adam, as the more important half of the partnership.

The manner of her taking leave of Adam -

> Thus saying, from her husband's hand her hand
> Soft she withdrew
>
> (IX, 385-6)

– is a wonderfully concentrated poetic moment, combining as it does physical sensation and psychological movement. The use of "Soft", which may be taken simultaneously as an adjective describing the texture of Eve's hand and as the adverb 'softly' denoting the manner of her withdrawal of it, also provides an ironic commentary on the steely resolution with which she acts. It would have been so easy to have portrayed this moment as an angry one, to have had Eve flouncing out to meet her just deserts. But Milton declines to do that. He has created her the queen of Eden's groves and he allows her to move out through them with "Goddess-like deport" to meet her fate.

When the crisis comes, Satan, as we see, makes light enough work of Eve. The less flexible mind of Adam, "Whose higher intellectual [i.e. intellect] more I shun" (IX, 483), as Satan admits to himself in choosing Eve as the target, would doubtless have played the Serpent's blandishments with the straight bat of obedience. Yet Satan does Eve the credit of advancing sophisticated arguments for eating the Apple. It is to her intellect that he appeals, and the Tree's promise of scientific, philosophical and moral understanding does appeal to her. As a, by now, thoroughly free-thinking Miltonist, she is bound to find that the Serpent's sudden attainment of the status of sentient being is an irresistible argument:

> look on me,
> Me, who have touched and tasted; yet both live,
> And life more perfect have attained than Fate
> Meant me, by venturing higher than my lot.
> Shall that be shut to Man, which to the Beast
> Is open?
>
> (IX, 687-92)

And there is the nicely judged appeal to envy. 'You are a human being, a lord of creation. You surely don't want to spend your life in a state of understanding lower than that of a serpent?'

In a sense it is not, at this point, Eve's problem, but Milton's. Eve must fall. That is the story he is under contract with God to tell us. But intellectually he cannot *explain* it to us. The stark necessity of obedience which functioned effectively enough in archetypal Genesis does not work as a categorical imperative in the psychologically more sophisticated atmosphere of *Paradise Lost*. God and his henchmen as portrayed by Milton have failed to make any case for *why* they should be obeyed. They dislike explanation and do not relish debate. Their rigid hierarchical thinking seems inadequate to comprehend the richness and complexity of the Creation, of which they are nevertheless in charge.

Is Eve, once having eaten the fruit, a different being? Perhaps she is, though on close inspection we might feel that any change is not really a qualitative one. Her rebellious mind now carries her thoughts on personal freedom and responsibility a stage further. She considers sharing her secret with Adam:

> Shall I to him make known
> As yet my change, and give him to partake
> Full happiness with me, or rather not,
> But keep the odds of knowledge in my power
> Without co-partner? so to add what wants
> In female sex, the more to draw his love,

> And render me more equal; and perhaps,
> A thing not undesirable, sometime
> Superior; for, inferior, who is free?
>
> (IX, 817-25)

As she ponders the future dynamics of their relationship a certain Machiavellian quality has entered her thinking. Yet it is not one that does discredit to her intelligence. It is her increased mental powers, "the odds of knowledge" on her side, not physical attractions she emphasises when thinking of what may now make her more lovable to Adam.

In the run-up to the tasting of the Apple, Milton has constantly editorialised on the folly of Eve's act. It will be "foul distrust, and breach/Disloyal" (IX, 6-7). At the crunch, Satan's persuasions "Into her heart too easy entrance won" (IX, 734) – though in fact we are shown her giving the matter strenuous thought. And when it happens, Nature "Sighing through all her works, gave signs of woe,/That all was lost." (IX, 783-4). Yet, as poet rather than catechist, he remains true to the vividly articulate Eve he has created. Her reflection, "for, inferior, who is free?" is an argument that might not have disgraced Satan at the top of his rhetorical form. And the delightful flash of jealousy that makes her in fact decide not to keep anything from Adam –

> but what if God have seen,
> And death ensue? then I shall be no more!
> And Adam, wedded to another Eve,
> Shall live with her enjoying
>
> (IX, 826-9)

– invests her with imperishable humanity and womanliness.

What should Adam have done? For C.S. Lewis there is absolutely no doubt in the matter:

> If conjugal love were the highest value in Adam's world, then of course his resolve [i.e. to fall with Eve] would have been the correct one. But if there are things that have an even higher claim on a man, if the universe is imagined to be such that, when the pinch comes, a man ought to reject wife and mother and his own life also, then the case is altered, and then Adam can do no good

> to Eve (as, in fact, he does no good) by becoming her accomplice
> ... The only thing Adam knows is that he must hold the fort, and
> he does not hold it.
>
> (A Preface to Paradise Lost, p.123)

Lewis' verdict draws us to the parallel with the plight of Christian at the outset of *The Pilgrim's Progress*. Now of course there is no doubt in our mind that Bunyan's protagonist must flee the things he loves in order "to be saved". But *Pilgrim's Progress* is an allegory. It exists on the plane of a moral and theological debate, and its 'characters' are states of mind and spirit, not fully fleshed human beings. By the time we have got as far as the Fall in *Paradise Lost* it would be far too late for Milton to reel in the humanity of his cast and make them allegorical ciphers, even if he wanted to.

To try an example from nearer our own time and experience: would one be justified in turning a husband/wife/loved one in to the authorities if one knew they were revealing secrets vital to the country's security to the enemy in a life-and-death struggle in wartime? And if the answer is yes, is Adam right to risk the future security of the entire universe all for an erring wife? The answer to that, too, might be yes. But is it ever made abundantly clear to Adam in *Paradise Lost*, in spite of all the hours of lecturing he endures from the management, that the Fall will have such calamitous consequences? Given that God in Heaven is frequently seen in a state of such great vexation on the subject, there appears to be scant trouble taken to acquaint Adam directly with all the likely consequences of disobedience. At the outset we see him hardly appearing to understand any of the consequences of God's injunction as he explains to Eve that they are

> not to taste that only tree
> Of knowledge, planted by the tree of life;
> So near grows death to life, whate'er death is,
> Some dreadful thing no doubt; for well thou knowest
> God hath pronounced it death to taste that tree.
>
> (IV, 423-7)

Adam does not even know what death means for the individual, much less that the whole happiness of the human race hangs on his and Eve's obedience. Perhaps Milton has forgotten that in Book VIII (later in the poem but earlier in its chronology – Adam is there recalling God's first words to him before Eve's creation) Adam understood that death will specifically mean that he will become mortal, and that he and Eve will be "expelled from hence into a world/Of woe and sorrow" (VIII, 332-3). When Adam comes to brief Eve on the subject in Book IV, it appears that he, too, has either forgotten or completely misunderstood what God had said about it.

It is left to Raphael to complete Adam's education on the subject. One has to say that, in four entire books in Adam's company (V-VIII), he doesn't seem to make a very thorough job of it. In his first approach to the subject, at the end of his account of the war in Heaven and the fall of the rebel angels, the archangel warns Adam "by dire example, to beware/Apostasy, by what befell in Heaven" (VII, 42-3). Poor Adam, reeling under a graphic account of a struggle between millions of warring angels, is hardly going to make a connection between these huge events and any hypothetical infringement of God's rules and regulations for them in their pleasant garden. As Milton makes clear, his thoughts are, rather, full of "admiration and deep muse, to hear/Of things so high and strange; things, to their thought/So unimaginable, as hate in Heaven" (VII, 52-4). What he is hungry to hear from Raphael at that moment is not the rule book for Eden, but chapter and verse on what God has been up to since the beginning of time.

As we have seen, this process has Raphael reacting to questions for long periods rather than dictating the exchanges between them. It is only as he leaves that the potential damage to Adam's posterity from eating the forbidden fruit is made anything like explicit, and that is rather thrown over the archangelic shoulder as he flies off, glad, as we think, to escape further inquisition from Adam on details of the sex life in heaven:

> take heed lest passion sway
> Thy judgement to do aught, which else free will
> Would not admit: thine, and of all thy sons,
> The weal or woe in thee is placed; beware!
>
> (VIII, 635-8)

Neither this, nor what has preceded it, amounts to anything like a detailed warning to Adam: that Satan has escaped from Hell; that he is quite definitely heading this way intent on mischief; and that the consequence for Adam and Eve of falling into any trap he may set will be expulsion from the Garden of Eden, eventual death and misery brought on all humanity for the foreseeable future – which is what God unequivocally ordered the archangel to tell them in Book V.

And it is made quite clear, as Adam ponders the yea or nay of following Eve's example and eating the Apple, that he is still not at all certain of what the precise consequences of the act may be. As we saw in Chapter 3 above, he takes refuge in the thought that God "would be loth/Us to abolish, lest the Adversary/Triumph" (IX, 946-8).

There is no metaphysical dimension in Adam's decision to fall with Eve. She was created for him, and he is in love with her. God will be angry, but exchanging her for the assurance of some future of bliss that he cannot really imagine, is simply not an option for him. She does not have to utter a word to persuade him. Milton the moralist may tell us that he is "fondly overcome with female charm" (IX, 999), but he has created too convincing a portrait of the relationship between the earthly pair for it to be dismissed in those terms. Adam's decision is made almost immediately after Eve tells him what she has done:

> How can I live without thee! how forgo
> Thy sweet converse, and love so dearly joined,
> To live again in these wild woods forlorn!
> Should God create another Eve, and I
> Another rib afford, yet loss of thee
> Would never from my heart. No, no! I feel
> The link of nature draw me: flesh of flesh,
> Bone of my bone thou art, and from thy state
> Mine never shall be parted, bliss or woe.
>
> (IX, 908-16)

These lines are the expression of a deep and profoundly understood love. Nothing of what we have seen of Heavenly affections can rival it. At the most crucial moment of the drama Milton puts into Adam's mouth one of the loveliest utterances in *Paradise Lost*. There is absolutely nothing he can do, with his moralist's hat on, to gainsay it.

What are we to make of the 'bad' sex that follows the Fall? Milton clearly wants us to think of it as reprehensible in a way that Adam and Eve's prelapsarian couplings were not. He has an uphill struggle on his hands. As so often when his heart is not actually in what he is proposing, the verse betrays a certain lack of conviction. The consumption of the Apple has, it would appear, imported a dimension of somehow deplorable lust into their traffic with each other, though from the ponderousness of Adam's flirting at this point we (indeed Eve) might be forgiven for not detecting it. His wordy exordium

> Eve, now I see thou art exact of taste,
> And elegant, of sapience no small part,
> Since to each meaning savour we apply,
> And palate call judicious ...
>
> (IX, 1017-20)

does not seem the most irresistible way to a woman's favours, though he does subsequently improve upon this to tell her she inflames his senses. Eve is made to reply with glances of "contagious fire". Milton's difficulty is that he cannot make postlapsarian sex sound radically different from its prelapsarian counterpart. Adam and Eve seem no more blameable than any couple who get randy with each other after a few drinks. A sort of drunkenness is, it seems, the only tangible effect of the Apple. Milton even forgets to downgrade the surroundings for this encounter. The consumption of their impulses is allowed to take place in a shaded bower on a couch of "Pansies and violets, and asphodel,/And hyacinth, earth's freshest softest lap" (IX, 1040-1). The bosom of nature is still as bountiful to them as it was in Book IV.

Nevertheless Milton wants to make the episode into a cardinal sin and he works hard to that end. The hangover from it is severe. Adam wakes from the sleep into which they both lapse like "Herculean Samson, from the harlot-lap/Of Philistean Dalilah [*sic*]" (IX, 1060-1). What Adam and Eve have done has left them apparently "destitute and bare/Of all their virtue" (IX, 1062-3). Adam will subsequently describe it indignantly to Eve as "foul concupiscence; whence evil store".

Eve has become a "harlot". (Here, as in his later *Samson Agonistes*, Milton gives the biblical Delilah no quarter.) The Apple-intoxicated sexual frolic has robbed the pair of all virtue. Future lovemaking will be tainted with "Our wonted ornaments [i.e. sexual organs] now soiled and stained" (IX, 1076). Adam now sees it as a sin that will store up evil not only for them but for the whole world in the future.

I can't help feeling that it is a pity that Milton chose to try to hang the discord that follows the Fall on this episode. For a man of his fastidious nature, he had actually done rather well in daring to be so explicit about passion in Eden. His departing from the Genesis story (and from St Augustine who could not believe that sex took place before the Fall) had quite fearlessly held up physical love between his earthly pair for our admiration as something natural, beautiful and enjoyable. In what precise way it has now somehow become 'dirty' is difficult to understand. Are we to imagine that until now their lovemaking lacked the animal heat it now seems to have acquired – which Milton suddenly wants to present to us as a 'bad' thing? It does not work. A single tipsy sex romp cannot be made to stand as a symbol for the entry of sin into the world, as Milton so desperately wants it to be.

By contrast, the vibrant contempt with which they settle in to blaming each other for what led to the Fall is invested with a psychological reality that is instantly recognisable. Adam's reproach to Eve

> Would thou hadst hearkened to my words, and staid
> With me, as I besought thee, when that strange
> Desire of wandering, this unhappy morn,
> I know not whence possessed thee; we had then
> Remained still happy
>
> (IX, 1134-8)

is the age-old cry of all husbands who are convinced that they 'know best' and that if only 'the wife' had listened to him things would have been all right. And Eve comes back at him with a logic that splendidly hedges its bets:

> Was I to have never parted from thy side?
> As good have grown there still a lifeless rib.
> Being as I am, why didst not thou, the head,
> Command me absolutely not to go,
> Going into such danger, as thou saidst?
>
> (IX, 1153-7)

Whichever one of these two contradictory propositions Adam attempts to answer, he will be in the wrong. Eve has lost none of her contrariness, nor the powers of argument that got her into trouble in the first place. It is wonderfully observed ding-dong stuff. Finally Adam is stung to fling in her face the nobleness of his act in a way that can only make him seem like a heel, as he reminds her that he "might have lived, and joyed immortal bliss,/Yet willingly chose rather death with thee" (IX, 1166-7). It is one of those domestic brawls from which neither participant can hope to emerge with credit. It is not pretty, but it is utterly convincing. Although Milton is here, as he was in the sex scene, in official 'disapproval mode' in relation to his two leading characters, he nevertheless cannot help allowing them to retain their unquenchable vitality.

6

Aftermath

The Adam and Eve who submit themselves to God's judgement in Book X are unrecognisable as the vital individuals who talked themselves into falling in Book IX. It is time the moral universe was got back on track. The poet has allowed his protagonists a humanity that is in danger of running away with the plot. It is a hangdog couple who present themselves to the Son, who here does the Father's work as the instrument of chastisement. (In so doing does he for the first time in the poem become a full-blown member of the Trinity, assuming God's authority rather than merely doing his bidding as a subordinate?)

Milton is at his least effective when compelled to a close adherence to Genesis. The famous biblical simplicity of God's demand "Where art thou?" has become something more wordy, less pithy:

> Where art thou, Adam, wont with joy to meet
> My coming seen far off? I miss thee here,
> Not pleased, thus entertained with solitude,
> Where obvious duty erewhile appeared unsought.
>
> (X, 103-6)

What is God/the Son saying? We have not had the slightest impression that he has been a regular visitor to Eden. Throughout he has stayed at a safe distance, nervily watching events from on high, exercising control from the celestial Command Centre through military patrols by Gabriel and his troops, and the diplomatic mission from Raphael.

A shamefaced Adam steps up to hear his fate and after an unattractively evasive apology gives the Son a completely erroneous account of his reasons for eating the Apple. "This Woman, whom thou madest to be my help/… Her doing seemed to justify the deed;/She gave me of the tree, and I did eat" (X, 137-43) is a straight falsification of the facts. The last line is virtually a direct quotation from the King James Bible. And that is Milton's problem here. What is true in the biblical account doesn't in any way do justice to Adam's motives in *Paradise Lost*. Why is he trying to hide behind Eve when, as we have seen, his decision to eat the Apple had nothing to do with any justification she might have provided, but was a reflex of pure love? He went into it open-eyed: "with thee/Certain my resolution is to die" (IX, 906-7).

Strangely, the – presumably omniscient – Son does not seem at all inclined to quarrel with Adam's account. It fits in neatly with his ready-made sermon: "Was she thy God, that her thou didst obey/Before his voice?" (X, 145-6). This, again, is a misrepresentation of events. Adam did not "obey" Eve. And the Son's patronising "Adorned/She was indeed, and lovely, to attract/Thy love, not thy subjection" (X, 151-3) – a man-to-man 'Look, she was just a pretty face, put here for your sexual pleasure. You weren't meant to listen to anything she said' – gives the impression that those in charge of Project Man have not bargained for the mental capacities of the beings they have created.

Eve likewise has nothing intelligent to say in her defence. She, too, lamely parrots Genesis. "The Serpent me beguiled, and I did eat" (X, 162). We hardly expected Adam and Eve to be brazenly defiant. But it is disappointing to hear them accepting God's strictures in a way that diminishes them and their motives. It is as if Milton the moralist had suddenly remembered that he must, after all, "justify the ways of God to men", and his own gloriously vibrant creations must now be subordinated to that credo.

Tellingly, when it is not his own inspiration driving his utterance, when he is, so to speak, 'copying' from his biblical sources, Milton's very control over his verse falls away:

> Because thou hast hearkened to the voice of thy wife,
> And eaten of the tree, concerning which
> I charged thee, saying, Thou shalt not eat thereof:
> Cursed is the ground for thy sake; thou in sorrow
> Shalt eat thereof, all the days of thy life;
> Thorns also and thistles it shall bring thee forth
> Unbid; and thou shalt eat the herb of the field.
>
> (X, 198-204)

Try reading this aloud and you will immediately feel how completely it fails to attain the confident rhythm of the Miltonic iambic pentameter that for so long and so successfully propels the argument of *Paradise Lost*. Only the second, third and fourth lines can be made to scan. The rest stumbles horribly, rhythmic emphasis falling where we least expect or want it. "Shalt eat thereof all the days of thy life", so trenchant in Genesis, becomes a horribly inadequate line when transposed unchanged into the poem. The poetic failure underscores the fact that the message, too, is an inadequate one. The thorny terms of the Genesis judgement are an incongruous sentence for this humanly complex Adam and Eve.

In the event, Adam redeems himself in our eyes before the end of Book X. There is a tender dignity in his sudden decision to end the recrimination that has soured his and Eve's relations with each other since the Fall. He does the right thing – forgives her:

> But rise, let us no more contend, nor blame
> Each other, blamed enough elsewhere; but strive
> In offices of love, how we may lighten
> Each other's burden, in our share of woe.
>
> (X, 958-61)

This is the instinctively unselfish love that enabled Adam to fall with Eve in the first place. Eve's response, though it is a wildly impractical one, is immensely appealing in its terms:

> Childless thou art, childless remain: so Death
> Shall be deceived his glut, and with us two
> Be forced to satisfy his ravenous maw.
> But if thou judge it hard and difficult,
> Conversing, looking, loving, to abstain
> From love's due rights, nuptial embraces sweet ...
> Then, both ourselves and seed at once to free
> From what we fear for both, let us make short;
> Let us seek Death, or he not found, supply
> With our own hands his office on ourselves.
>
> (X, 989-1002)

In other words: 'Let us remain childless, so depriving Death of his desired prey – the entire human race. But, if you think you will find it impossible to keep your hands off me, with consequences that will inevitably defeat this resolve, let's kill ourselves.' Magnanimity is met with magnanimity. We know that there is not the slightest chance that Eve's proposition will be taken up by Adam, but there is a sweet striving for level-headedness about her that goes straight to our hearts.

Not even *Paradise Lost*'s most unconditional apologists have been able to find much to praise in Books XI and XII – until that is we are brought to the immortal final lines of the poem which propel the fallen couple out of Paradise. Milton's young acquaintance Thomas Ellwood, who took the cottage in Chalfont St Giles in Buckinghamshire that enabled him to complete *Paradise Lost* at a safe distance from plague-ridden London, and was the first man to be allowed to read it, is reported to have said to its author: "Thou has said much here of *Paradise Lost*; what hast thou to say of Paradise found?" The direct result of Ellwood's challenge was of course *Paradise Regained*. This long-winded exegesis of the New Testament temptation of Christ, to which topic it, strangely, confines itself, nowhere achieves the largeness or level of inspiration of its predecessor.

Perhaps, like many readers since, Ellwood's stamina failed him before he got to Book XII. He seems not to have noticed that *Paradise Lost* has in fact a great deal to say about biblical events leading up to and including the redemption of Man through Christ's sacrifice on the Cross. We would really rather it hadn't. Even that doughty defender C.S. Lewis could find little merit in the epic's last two books: "Such an untransmuted lump of futurity, coming in a position so momentous for the structural effect of the whole work, is inartistic." Lewis is surprised that the writing in these two books is "curiously bad". But there is little to be surprised at in that. As we have seen on several occasions, where Milton lacks inspiration, so does his poetry. In Books XI and XII it has a dogged, pedestrian quality.

It falls to the Archangel Michael to deliver the Milton Lecture on the Future of Mankind to his one-man audience. Perhaps the stern warrior-prince of Heaven was not the right choice for this intellectual undertaking, though his presence at this point is a structural necessity, since it is clearly appropriate that he rather than any of his fellow angels shall drive Adam and Eve from Eden.

The technique of a narrative within a narrative is germane to epic poetry. Both Homer and Virgil employ it. But a detailed résumé of the contents of the Old Testament was always bound to be heavy going. Adam, reduced merely to the role of reacting at convenient pauses in Michael's account, cuts a sorry figure. We see him feebly echoing the archangel's moral commentary on the Bible story.

The mating of the "sons of God" with the "daughters of men", as reported in Genesis 6:4, is characteristic. Michael recreates this as a vision of lovemaking which Adam is at first inclined to interpret as a portent of happier things ahead for mankind. "Here Nature seems fulfilled in all her ends" (XI, 602). Michael slaps him down: "Judge not what is best/By pleasure, though to nature seeming meet" (XI, 603-4). Adam falls dutifully into line. "O pity and shame, that they, who to live well/Entered so fair, should turn aside to tread/Paths indirect" (XI, 629-31). He appears to be becoming a thoroughgoing prig under Michael's unwholesome influence.

We next see him in a state of pitiful gratitude over the eventual 'happy ending' to the story in Michael's account of the redemption. "O Goodness infinite, Goodness immense!/That all this good of evil shall produce,/And evil turn to good" (XII, 469-71).

We have finally arrived at the "Fortunate Fall" hinted at by Milton almost at the outset of Book I. Of course, doctrinally, Milton had to believe in such an optimistic outcome. But Genesis had him under no obligation to arm Adam with a consolation that tends to undermine his poem. Given the magnitude of the spiritual journey we have made through *Paradise Lost*, such a resolution as this is bound to seem absurd:

> Full of doubt I stand,
> Whether I should repent me now of sin
> By me done, and occasioned; or rejoice
> Much more, that much more good thereof shall spring;
> To God more glory, more good-will to Men.
>
> (XII, 473-7)

There hasn't, apparently, been a problem after all. Everything is going to be all right. If Milton had left it there this would have provided a truly bathetic conclusion to a mighty mental effort. Fortunately he doesn't. He stages a finale which surely puts beyond doubt the answer to the question of who the heroes of *Paradise Lost* really are. It is somehow fitting that the last words spoken in the poem are given to Eve, whose innate spirit of rebellious enquiry has propelled the drama from Book V onwards. In a last great effort, Milton restores dignity and independence to his human pair in an imperishable image:

> Some natural tears they dropt, but wiped them soon;
> The World was all before them, where to choose
> Their place of rest, and Providence their guide:
> They, hand in hand, with wand'ring steps and slow,
> Through Eden took their solitary way.
>
> (XII, 645-9)

The angels have gone, retired behind Eden's gate, from where they look on, oddly reduced in stature to "dreadful faces thronged" (XII, 644). The Miltonic verse, flaccid and prosy throughout so much of these last two books, recovers its verve at the very end. It is as if Milton himself comes to life again when left in the sole company of this heroic pair. We would not wish them back in "Paradise so late their happy seat".

What had happened to Milton during the composition of *Paradise Lost*, concluded in the first decade of the Restoration amid the utter ruin of all his hopes? Is it a case of sheer creative exhaustion? Or had he lost faith in the vision of the Puritan revolution which, as a devout believer, he had been inclined to associate with a sign of God's particular grace bestowed on the English race? The Commonwealth, too, had stumbled. His hero on earth, Cromwell, had emerged as a dictator, whose edicts Milton nevertheless was obliged to defend in detail, until the return of a monarchy he deeply despised relieved him of this hopeless task.

We feel that the promise of salvation to Adam as the poem's final solution, can give Milton the poet no real consolation. In *Paradise Lost* he pays lip-service to what he clearly regards as the admirable principle of authority. Obedience, as he had made clear in *De Doctrina*, is the watchword, and it is the failure to obey in one apparently cardinal instance that is the ruination of mankind. But as a poet he can never make that principle convince. His Heaven remains inert, while the libertarian Milton unwittingly bestows his affections elsewhere. Adam and Eve will be forgiven through the Redemption, but that remote promise seems as nothing beside the forgiveness for each other that they find within themselves. In spite of himself, Milton preserves to the end of *Paradise Lost* a republic of the spirit, and it is this that Adam and Eve take with them as they leave Eden for that world which lies "all before them" in its splendour and mystery.

7

The Poetry of *Paradise Lost*

At various points in this narrative we have paused to examine the ways in which Milton obtains his poetic effect in particular instances. Perhaps more than with any other poet the authorial style is regarded as integral to – and vital to the success or failure of – the 'message'. As we have seen, where Milton appears to lack perfect conviction his verse reflects that.

It is generally accepted that the style of *Paradise Lost* is a rather lofty one. That expectation was articulated in the title of Christopher Ricks' study *Milton's Grand Style* (1963), though in fact that intelligent and persuasive book went on to analyse a host of other attributes of the verse. But it is not only we, in an age that requires communication to be instant, who may have to draw a deep breath before engaging with a medium like Milton's. Dr Johnson, himself a man of some sonority, pronounced it wearisome. Milton's contemporaries and near contemporaries were keenly alive to the difficulties he presents. In his *Explanatory Notes and Remarks on Paradise Lost* (1734) the artist and critic Jonathan Richardson conceded that "Milton's language is English, but 'tis Milton's English; 'tis Latin, 'tis Greek English."

Yes, Milton sometimes gives the impression of wishing that English had been, like Latin and Greek, an inflected language. Indeed he often wrote it as if it were so, placing adjectives and adverbs in splendid if ambiguous isolation, making us puzzle over whether one is not in fact the other, and leaving main verbs suspended for long periods before bringing them into action and revealing his meaning. The following is characteristic of such difficulties:

> And they, who to be sure of Paradise,
> Dying, put on the weeds of Dominick,
> Or in Franciscan think to pass disguised;
> They pass the planets seven, and pass the fixed,

> And that crystalling sphere whose balance weighs
> The trepidation talked, and that first moved.
>
> (III, 478-83)

Milton is never at his best in a digression, and certainly not in a digression which is devoted to a sideswipe at the Roman Catholic Church and other pet hates and perceived heresies. We may get the general gist, even if we are not immediately party to the contemporary detail of the cosmos with which Milton is familiar. But to the end it remains unclear just what parts of speech – verbs, participles, adjectives – 'weighs', 'talked' and 'moved' are. Language is becoming a private code, and meaning runs into the sand. Had this been Latin, the case endings of the words would have immediately told us what their functions were.

As we have seen, Milton gave serious thought to writing his epic in Latin. There is perhaps something slightly ridiculous about such a poet hesitating on such a question, given that Shakespeare had amply demonstrated through his great tragedies that English had the power to carry off the loftiest of subjects in a manner that proud contemporaries could boast rivalled the best efforts of antiquity.

But this author of much Latin verse remained a little under the influence of that feeling which had in an early poem 'At a Vacation Exercise in the College' given rise to the sentiment "Hail native language that by sinews weak/Didst move my first endeavouring tongue to speak." It is as if he felt that English, in adhering to a word order, was a somehow cruder vehicle than the inflected classical languages, rather than being, as it is, a marvellous instrument in its simple grammar and powerful syntax.

In his prefatory note on his epic Milton made something of an issue of his use of blank verse – "English heroic verse without rhyme", as he called it – as the poetic medium of *Paradise Lost*. He cited Homer and Virgil as his models, and castigated rhyme "in longer works especially" as "the invention of a barbarous age to set off wretched matter". Again, Shakespeare and his contemporaries had already demonstrated the power and flexibility of blank verse, and the world in general has not taken issue with Milton on his decision.

As we shall see in the next chapter, T.S. Eliot decided that Milton's style, because it moved away from the speech-derived poetic of Shakespeare and the Jacobean dramatists, was a 'bad' one – as if there were any requirement for poetry to be the language of speech. Eliot was later to revise this opinion to conclude that "the remoteness of Milton's verse from ordinary speech, his invention of his own poetic language, seems to me one of the marks of his greatness".

As it happens, where Milton is inspired by one of his characters he is quite capable of making them speak in a psychologically consistent and realistic way, as he does with Satan and the rebel angels and (at least intermittently), with Adam and Eve. This is of course not the same thing as saying that he would have made a good dramatist. There would have been too many, too long, speeches.

Milton's style can be any one of a number of things. It can be massively sonorous as it is in his unforgettably splendid opening to *Paradise Lost*:

> Of Man's first disobedience, and the fruit
> Of that forbidden tree whose mortal taste
> Brought death into the World, and all our woe,
> With loss of *Eden*, till one greater Man
> Restore us, and regain the blissful seat,
> Sing, Heavenly Muse.
>
> (I, 1-6)

This, we immediately feel, is the way a great epic should begin. Like the opening of the *Iliad* and *Aeneid* it proposes its matter with irresistible force. This first sentence extends over sixteen lines without at all taxing our powers of endurance or understanding. In the second we are borne along to line 26 and Milton's tremendous opening proposition, namely that he will, his muse assenting, "assert Eternal Providence,/And justify the ways of God to men". Meaning is sustained throughout in a single magnificent cadence.

The poetry can be exquisitely lyrical, as it is when Milton's enraptured gaze is held in a moment of sheer love for his earthly pair.

> These, lulled by nightingales, embracing slept,
> And on their naked limbs the flowery roof
> Showered roses, which the morn repaired.
>
> (IV, 771-3)

Keats might have envied such lines.

In a completely different vein Milton is capable of delivering a succession of verbal blows, as he does to convey the jolting discomfort of terrain, here experienced by the aimlessly wandering angels in the abyss:

> O'er many a frozen, many a fiery alp,
> Rocks, caves, lakes, fens, bogs, dens, and shades of death –
> A universe of death.
>
> (II, 620-2)

Each of the ten syllables of the second quoted line is a word. The line itself is inordinately long, both visually and when read aloud, and communicates an almost physical impression of unending and futile toil. It is a sense of discomfort that works, remarkably, even though we know that these are spirits and the landscape is a purely conceptual one.

In a place so difficult to describe as Heaven with its intangible attributes, the poetry functions most effectively when it operates in generalities, and stays at some distance from its subject. Satan's starry hosts seen approaching from afar impress with a sense of incalculable menace. Satan and his followers at close quarters busying themselves in the manufacture of artillery with which to discomfit the angels during the war in Heaven present us with insuperable incongruities:

> sulphurous and nitrous foam
> They found, they mingled, and, with subtle art,
> Concocted and adusted they reduced
> To blackest grain, and into store conveyed:
> Part hidden veins digged up (nor hath this earth
> Entrails unlike) of mineral and stone,
> Whereof to found their engines and their balls
> Of missive ruin
>
> (VI, 512-19)

It is a valiant attempt, but the geology and chemistry become an incubus whose burden is reflected in the turgidity of the verse. The bracket only exacerbates the problems of a syntax which is here always in danger of losing its grip on the intended meaning. The logistics of celestial warfare, like the mechanics of angelic sex, present, in the end, an impossible challenge to Milton's technical resources.

Fleshing out God and his followers involves Milton in even greater difficulties. This is God seen in majesty:

> About him all the Sanctities of Heaven
> Stood thick as stars, and from his sight receiv'd
> Beatitude past utterance.
>
> (III, 60-2)

If he had been able to sustain something like this Milton might, one feels, have provided a consistently convincing vision of Heaven. But the perils of venturing too close are exemplified in his description of an angelic banquet which follows the announcement that the Son is to become God's all-powerful vicegerent.

> Tables are set, and on a sudden piled
> With Angels' food, and rubied nectar flows
> In pearl, in diamond, and massy gold,
> Fruit of delicious vines, the growth of Heaven.
> On flowers reposed, and with fresh flowerets crowned,
> They eat, they drink
>
> (V, 632-7)

What is the objection? The verse itself is vigorous enough. But Milton has injected into the proceedings a meaning he may not have intended. There is something unbecoming in the spectacle of these angels enjoying the pleasures of the table and the flowing cup. We seem to have toppled over into something perilously close to gluttony. And the feeling is amplified by the fact that the repast and accompanying drinks are served from gold and gem-encrusted vessels. We expect splendour but not luxury in Heaven. There is certainly no precedent for this in the Old Testament. The scene is in marked and unpleasant contrast with the dignified moderation of Adam and Eve's reception of Raphael earlier in this book. (Is there also lurking unease in the implication that the angels have been somehow 'bought off' by this luxury in compensation for their earlier acquiescence in surrendering all their powers to the Son?)

This might, for all the world, be a Titian bacchanal.

Which brings us to one of Milton's difficulties as the poet of a Christian epic. He is simply steeped in, and in love with, classical mythology. The grim backdrop of the Old Testament cannot furnish him with the glowing colours and wealth of incident he needs to weave the rich tapestry of *Paradise Lost*. As we saw in Book V, Eve in Eden effortlessly became the classical Goddess of Love, as if Milton could not resist it, when decorum surely cried out at that point for her to be behaving like the Mother of Mankind and the ancestor of the Virgin Mary.

Of course any Christian poet is entitled to invoke in a general way the assistance of the Muses, simply from a consciousness of his operating in the classical epic framework. But Milton is forced constantly to classical mythology in search of the tools he needs to make his poetic landscape as vivid as he wants it to be. In the very opening such hardy perennial reference points in the biblical landscape as Mt Horeb (Sinai), Sion hill, and Siloa's brook are paraded before us, as Milton alludes to Moses the lawgiver and pastoral shepherd of his flock. But Moses cannot be used to serve as bard. When Milton wants, so to speak, to put his marker down for the scale of the enterprise he is about to attempt, it is to classical mythology that he instinctively turns:

> I thence
> Invoke thy aid to my adventurous song,
> That with no middle flight intends to soar
> Above th' Aonian mount, while it pursues
> Things unattempted yet in prose or rhyme
>
> (I, 12-16)

The Aonian mount is synonymous with Mt Helicon, home of the Greek muses, and source of the stream Hippocrene, struck from the rock by the hoof of Pegasus to be the eternal source of inspiration to all poets. This is Milton's natural dwelling place.

One of the most celebrated instances of Milton's recourse to classical mythology occurs at the very moment he is endeavouring to impress on us the beauties of the biblical Eden as Satan, in cormorant guise, surveys it from his vantage point on the top of the Tree of Life. Milton has already furnished us with many lines of conventional description of which the following may stand as an example:

> Betwixt them lawns, or level downs, and flocks
> Grazing the tender herb, were interposed,
> Or palmy hillock; or the flowery lap
> Of some irriguous valley spread her store.
>
> (IV, 252-5)

As description it is serviceable enough, but there is something mechanical and essentially inert about it. Its "level downs", "tender herb" and "flowery lap" are selected from a ready-made stock of pastoral epithets. (The Latinity of "irriguous valley" is decidedly more Miltonic, though it is actually not his coinage.) In any event Paradise would never have taken such root in our minds had Milton left it like this. But he suddenly has a flash of inspiration:

> Not that fair field
> Of Enna, where Proserpine gathering flowers,
> Herself a fairer flower by gloomy Dis
> Was gathered, which cost Ceres all that pain
> To seek her through the world ...
> ... might with this Paradise
> Of Eden strive
>
> (IV, 268-75)

Why bring in Ceres like this, only to rebuff her? we may ask ourselves. And yet the effect of this glancing shaft is strangely arresting. Milton builds up an apparently disconnected classical allusion alongside his major theme – and then makes it emotionally stand for it. Yet that effect is apparently achieved by a downright denial. The Vale of Enna in Sicily cannot, we are assured, rival Eden in beauty. Yet in being pronounced superior to that "fair field" and its crowd of mythological associations, Eden, until now a blank sheet or at best an insipid still life, has suddenly become a much more interesting place. Its inhabitants will be invested by association with those of classical myth, with their capacity to experience godlike sorrow. When we think of Eden, the memory of Ceres and her pain at losing her daughter to the king of the underworld will haunt us, long after its level downs and flowery lap are forgotten. The apparently 'negative' comparison takes us into the future and foreshadows the pain that Eve, like Ceres, will know when it becomes her turn to have traffic with the lord of darkness. By approaching his subject tangentially like this, Milton achieves a complexity which gives us one of the most poignant images of *Paradise Lost*. In such moments as this, Milton the Maker is simply incomparable.

8

Critical Fortunes

Milton's status as one of the giants of literature has not always, like that of Shakespeare, been above dispute. Unlike Shakespeare's, that reputation depends, effectively, on a single work, his *chef d'oeuvre*, *Paradise Lost*. In introducing Shakespeare to the world, a few years after his death in a dedicatory poem printed with the First Folio of his works issued in 1623, Ben Jonson, a man notoriously jealous of Shakespeare in his lifetime, had nevertheless magnanimously conceded the verdict on his great rival that has never been revised: "He was not of an age but for all time!" And at the same time he somewhat jingoistically allowed his fellow countryman to have surpassed "all that insolent Greece or haughty Rome put forth".

A commendatory poem by Milton's contemporary Andrew Marvell, which prefaces the second edition of *Paradise Lost*, published in 1674, makes a very different impression on us. Marvell clearly *meant* to praise his friend and former colleague – and substantially he does so. Yet his eulogy is shot through, perhaps unconsciously, with moments of unease, little hesitations of the kind that have tended to surface over the subsequent centuries of criticism: "I liked his project, the success did fear – /Through that wide field how he his way should find …/Lest he perplexed the things he would explain." As he reads on it all turns out right for an anxious Marvell in the end: "Thou hast not missed one thought that could be fit/And all that was improper dost omit"; "Thy verse created like thy verse sublime,/In number, weight and measure, needs not rhyme." But it all amounts to a species of praise that inhabits a plane some way below the unforced exaltation of Jonson. We are left with the feeling that Marvell has had to work hard to admire – and perhaps did not much enjoy – *Paradise Lost*.

And so it has continued down the ages. Both Milton's subject matter and his style have caused difficulties. The retelling of a Bible story whose fundamentals are so embedded in a Christian culture and may be assumed to brook no embroidery of the facts, was always going to be a hazardous undertaking. And to do it in poetry that in places appears to derive its life from academic study, and its syntax from classical languages, was always in danger of compounding the difficulties.

As early as 1693, Milton's younger contemporary John Dryden, who had previously described Milton as combining the virtues of Homer and Virgil, was identifying some of the difficulties both of matter and form: "It is true that he runs into a flat of thought, sometimes for a hundred lines together, but it is when he has got into a track of scripture." And he reminds us: "His antiquated words were his choice, not his necessity" (*A Discourse Concerning the Original and Progress of Satire*). In 1723 Alexander Pope was echoing much the same concerns in his *Postscript to the Odyssey*: "there is frequently such transposition and forced construction that the very sense is not to be discovered without a second or third reading: and in this certainly he ought to be no example." The notion of the bad example supposedly set by Milton in his poetic method was to be a recurrent theme among critics. Significantly it occurs most especially among those who are practising poets, who recoil in alarm at the thought either of attempting the Miltonic style themselves or of the pernicious influence it may have on them if they immerse themselves too thoroughly in it.

Yet, almost contemporaneously, in France, Voltaire, who had been unable to stomach what he saw as the barbarities of Shakespeare, came riding to the support of England's epic poet in his *Essay upon the Civil Wars of France, extracted from Curious Manuscripts and also upon the Epick Poetry of the European Nations from Homer down to Milton* (1727): "There is something above the reach of human forces to have attempted the creation without bombast." For Voltaire "The meanness (if there is any) of some parts of the subject is lost in the immensity of the poetical invention."

It was for Samuel Johnson, in his essay on Milton in *Lives of the English Poets* (1779) to make, as he so often did, the most influential pronouncement of his century on *Paradise Lost*. Conservative politically, socially and in matters of religion, Johnson was of course instinctively at odds with most of what the republican, Presbyterian and free-thinking Milton stood for. But where his prejudices do not get the better of his judgement he makes telling points that can always be usefully paraded as evidence for the prosecution in the continuing debate on *Paradise Lost*. Such astute analyses as that of the unhappy mix of allegory and reality in the meeting between Satan, Sin and Death in Book II, or what he astutely identified as "the confusion of spirit and matter which pervades the whole narrative of the war in heaven", are worth reading again, even when we do not agree with them. The massive Johnsonian self-assurance of his final verdict on the poem, "Its perusal is a duty rather than a pleasure," has, alas, been far too persuasive on faint hearts down the ages.

The Romantics took enthusiastically to *Paradise Lost*. William Blake's famous assertion in *The Marriage of Heaven and Hell* (1793) that "The reason Milton wrote in fetters when he wrote of Angels & God, and at liberty when of Devils & Hell, is because he was a true poet and of the Devil's party without knowing it" was to become something of a rallying cry to the age (though it was actually Dryden who had first suggested that Satan might in fact be Milton's hero). Yet there was fierce disagreement among the poets themselves as to where the precise merits of *Paradise Lost* lay. For Coleridge (in marked contrast to Dryden and Johnson) "Every word is to the purpose. There are no lazy intervals: all has been considered and demands and merits observation" (*Notes*, 1797). Coleridge later acknowledged gloomily: "I wish the *Paradise Lost* were more carefully read and studied than I can see any ground for believing it is." But for Keats (speaking admittedly as a poet, and one who had failed horribly when attempting his own epic, *Hyperion*, along Miltonic lines) the verse of *Paradise Lost* was "a corruption of our language ... I have but lately stood on my guard against Milton. Life to him would be death to me" (Letter to George and Georgiana Keats, 1819).

For Wordsworth (in whom, even in his Romantic fervour, there always lurked a Miltonic quality) Milton was an almost Messianic figure whose Second Coming could not be ushered in a moment too soon:

> Milton! Thou shouldst be living at this hour:
> England hath need of thee: she is a fen
> Of stagnant waters: altar, sword, and pen,
> Fireside, the heroic wealth of hall and bower
> Have forfeited their ancient English dower

Of inward happiness. We are selfish men;
Oh! raise us up, return to us again.

It makes strange reading. Wordsworth, here, is not as he later became, the hardened conservative who could pen with all the best intentions the grisly *Sonnets upon the Punishment of Death* of 1841, but is writing in 1802 with English literature's Romantic age opening before him in its first flush, and his own best work yet to come. Yet he invokes the spirit of Milton not as the author of the beauties of *L'Allegro* and *Il Penseroso* and the splendours of *Paradise Lost*, but as some grim Puritan warrior, required to cleanse the Augean stables of English life.

As the liberal experiments and the artistic excitement of the Romantic period gradually gave way to the Victorian age with its public adherence to austerer virtues and greater certainties, Milton's heroic simplicity and solid morals were increasingly appreciated, ensuring a continuing popularity for *Paradise Lost*. Thus, Matthew Arnold in an address on Milton in St Margaret's Church, Westminster in 1888, speaks not so much as a literary critic, but rather as someone looking for a hero to whom he can turn to get the nation out of a tight corner:

> If to our English race an inadequate sense for perfection in work is a real danger, if the discipline of respect for a high and flawless excellence is particularly needed by us, Milton is of all our gifted men the best lesson, the most salutary influence.

The 20th century, especially as it took shape after the shock of the First World War, with the birth of a new scepticism, and the beginnings of what we might call modern literary criticism, made it difficult to 'enlist', as it were, a literary figure and his work in this way. The century was soon to usher in the most radical and relentless devaluation of Milton's reputation that had occurred to that point. That it was conducted by two minds of unimpeachable quality made it the more formidable and effective. The poet T.S. Eliot and the Cambridge academic F.R. Leavis managed in only a few pages of comment not merely to suggest, but almost, it seemed, to *prove*, that Milton had all along been overrated and that he did not merit the position of eminence he had been accorded in English literature.

The attack, which was directed rather at the nature of the poetry of *Paradise Lost*, than its content, had been opened in an essay of 1921 by T.S. Eliot which commended the newly published *Metaphysical Lyrics and Poems of the Seventeenth Century: Donne to Butler* edited by Herbert Grierson. In this essay, 'The Metaphysical Poets', Eliot ascribed to "the two most powerful poets of the century, Milton and Dryden" (an odd linking of two very different figures) what he called "a dissociation of sensibility" that, according to him, had "set in" to English poetry from the middle of the 17th century onwards. By this Eliot meant that, under the influence of these master stylistic showmen, words gradually lost their power to express feelings simply and directly, as they had done in the works of the poets and playwrights of the Elizabethan and Jacobean periods, and their predecessors. The verse became more elaborate and artificial, the sensibility cruder. Thus, according to Eliot (and persuasively demonstrated by him), by the time we arrive at the poetry of Tennyson and Browning, an almost complete divorce between the vigour of speech as it is heard and verse on the page has taken place.

Eliot elaborated what he meant, this time focusing his charge solely on Milton, in an essay *Milton: Style and Tradition* (1936). Of *Paradise Lost* he hazarded:

> A disadvantage of the rhetorical style appears to be, that a dislocation takes place through the hypertrophy of the auditory imagination at the expense of the visual and tactile, so that the inner meaning is separated from the surface, and tends to become something occult, or at least without effect on the reader until fully understood.

Eliot also took issue with what he described as the "repellent" theology of *Paradise Lost*, "expressed through a mythology which would have better been left in the Book of *Genesis*, on which Milton has not improved". (A crucial question, as we have seen, but one on which Eliot was to back-track as a 'believer' in 1947.)

In his immensely influential book *Revaluation*, published later in 1936, F.R. Leavis set his imprimatur on the position as he saw it:

Milton's dislodgement, in the past decade, after his two centuries of predominance, was effected with remarkably little fuss. The irresistible argument was, of course, Mr Eliot's creative achievement; it gave his few critical asides – potent it is true by context – their finality, and made it unnecessary to elaborate a case.

There was, as it were, a QED, in the tone of this, which gave it the apparent unassailablity of the proof of a mathematical theorem.

It may be thought astonishing that in the radical process of dethroning such a figure as Milton, a man of Leavis' manifest rigour found it "unnecessary to elaborate a case". But so it was. The phrase "dissociation of sensibility" caught on and was wielded as a touchstone for understanding the difference between the 'good' and the 'bad' in English poetry. Generations of university undergraduates, lecturers and school teachers were affected by the edicts of these two powerful witnesses for the prosecution.

The effect of this iconoclasm was not entirely pernicious. It went well beyond the question of Milton's style. Unquestioning reverence for *Paradise Lost* was replaced by a lively and intelligent debate on the merits of Milton's epic from all points of view. This, in an age when Christian belief itself was being subjected to much examination, led healthily to the central question of what, in fact, Milton had *meant* in his version of the Creation, Eden and the Fall. In this process such committed Christians as C.S. Lewis (*A Preface to Paradise Lost*) pleaded against Leavis, but found themselves joined in the arena by avowed atheists like the poet and critic William Empson (*Milton's God*). Milton's epic was subjected to a particularly unsparing scrutiny by A.J.A. Waldock, whose persuasive survey *Paradise Lost and its Critics*, with its stimulating scepticism, asked more questions of Milton's control over his material in *Paradise Lost* than, it seemed, could be comfortably answered. Milton's permanent reputation, in fact, seemed likely to be in far greater danger from Waldock's enquiry, conducted as it was in a sympathetic and genuinely engaged spirit, than it had been from the dismissive tone of Eliot and Leavis.

More recent criticism, with its tendency to focus on text independent of its context, or to take us in too minute detail into specific areas, lacks perhaps some of the robust forthrightness and intellectual excitement of its forebears. Among characteristic approaches we find: "This eccentric textual subject, the womb of meaning that exceeds the masculine will of its author so that he may enjoy and regain himself, constitutes, as it were, the free will of the text" (Marshall Grossman, 'The Genders of God and the Redemption of the Flesh in *Paradise Lost*', in *Milton and Gender*, ed. Catherine Gimelli Martin); or "Whenever we appropriate the poem for our own textual politics, we exploit Eve as text object", (Diane McColley, 'Eve and the Arts of Eden', in *Milton and the Idea of Woman*, ed. Julia M. Walker). Such approaches as these seem to me to shy away from the ideas a student would like to be grappling with as he or she prowls about before this formidable edifice of a poem, and the majestic beings who inhabit it.

What is surprising in an era when one might have thought Christianity to be further declined in influence, is its apparent resurgence as a force to be reckoned with among critics of *Paradise Lost*. This may be something to do with the fact that a huge volume of critical work on Milton and *Paradise Lost* has been generated by academic institutions in the United States, where Christianity is in a much healthier state than it is here, where indeed faith is often taken as a given. Thus McColley, a professor of English at Rutgers University, can say – apropos an injunction to "recognise and love goodness of which Adam and Eve are both brimful":

> The cure is to exercise a principle of interpretation Milton calls "candour: whereby we cheerfully acknowledge the gifts of God in our neighbour and interpret all his [her] words in a favourable sense" – unless he [she] attempts to "seduce or deter us from the love of God and true religion".

(Colley's quotation is from *De Doctrina Christiana*.) This sort of thinking does appear to give literary criticism a new and extraordinary remit – but it will not get us very far in trying to determine the meaning of *Paradise Lost*.

The tendency to want to see *Paradise Lost* as a sermon or source of spiritual guidance rather than as a work of art, is also present in recent criticism published in the United Kingdom, where religious faith is an undoubtedly weaker commodity than it is in America. Thus, in *Milton:*

Poet, Pamphleteer and Patriot, in countering Blake's provocative assertion that Milton was "of the Devil's party without knowing it", Anna Beer takes refuge in the idea that:

> Milton, far from losing control of his anti-hero, has designed him so that the reader falls for Satan's lies, is solicitous for his psychological torment and is seduced by his charisma. Only at the end of the poem does the reader, shame-facedly realise that this has been a mis-reading. That moment of realisation is also a moment in which the reader recognises his or her own sin. *Paradise Lost's* entrapment of the reader is, however, no negative game, but one that encourages readers to learn from their responses, and thus to renew their moral vigilance.

Now no one for a moment denies that great literature can be a source of moral enlightenment for its readers. But I can't think that even a stout moralist like Milton would have been easy with such a prescriptive definition of his art as Beer gives us here.

* * *

In conclusion, how successful is *Paradise Lost* at achieving what it sets out to do, and how are we to estimate its ultimate merits? As we have seen, it has undoubted flaws, and it seems to me best that these are admitted as such, and not somehow enlisted as virtues and used as tools to demonstrate that Milton was at all points in the poem in control of the message and the means of transmitting it.

As a poet Milton found spiritual grandeur in places he might not have expected, and that perception was at times to be at loggerheads with his theology, and its demand for unquestioning obedience to an omnipotent deity. He manifestly failed to justify the ways of God to men. But that does not mean that *Paradise Lost* is therefore a failure. Nor does it seem to me that the poem is, as it has often been characterised, a flawed masterpiece. I prefer to think of it as a masterpiece with flaws, and one that can, notwithstanding them, stand comparison with any of its kind in world literature.

Milton, with his unshakeable belief in the potential of rational man to find solutions to guide his way through this puzzling world, was always going, in spite of himself, to reveal the heroes of his epic, not among the celestial beings, not even in the Son the Redeemer, not among Satan and his angels, magnificent as they are, but in his earthly characters. These are the beings that his immensely humane spirit really understands. In creating such a pair and placing them in such a theological drama as this is, he took fearful risks. But he gave his Adam and Eve what none of the other characters possesses, a memorable beauty of soul. Their final dismissal from the gates of Paradise "hand in hand, with wand'ring steps and slow" is Milton's enduring testimony to human faith, decency, courage and love.

Further Reading

Critical and biographical studies
Anna Beer, *Milton: Poet, Pamphleteer and Patriot* (Bloomsbury, 2008). A quatercentenary offering that is useful rather than inspiring.

A.E. Dyson and Julian Lovelock (eds.), *Milton: Paradise Lost* (Macmillan, 1973). A well chosen collection of essays in the publisher's Casebook paperback series. They provide comment and criticism from the 17th century to the editors' own essay written in the year of publication.

T.S. Eliot, *Selected Essays* (Faber and Faber, 1951); *On Poetry and Poets* (Faber and Faber, 1957). The first contains the review of Grierson's edition of the Metaphysical poets which famously coined the concept of "dissociation of sensibility" as a criticism of Milton, the second, the maturer Eliot's retraction.

William Empson, *Milton's God* (Chatto & Windus, 1961). Quirky and provocative performance by English criticism's most famous atheist. Not surprisingly he is very good on Satan.

Frank Kermode (ed.), *The Living Milton* (Routledge & Kegan Paul, 1960). A collection of especially commissioned essays reflecting some of the concerns of mid-20th-century critics and scholars.

F.R. Leavis, *Revaluation* (Chatto & Windus, 1936). Witness for the prosecution, and a most formidable one. Although widely disagreed with these days, he is far too intelligent not to be still worth reading.

C.S. Lewis, *A Preface to Paradise Lost* (Oxford University Press, 1942). An impassioned apologia for the poem, written with knowledge and love.

Catherine Gimelli Martin (ed.), *Milton and Gender* (Cambridge University Press, 2004). Contemporary essays by American critics, focusing on Milton's attitudes towards women both in his life and as they emerge from his works.

Christopher Ricks, *Milton's Grand Style* (Oxford University Press, 1963). Thorough and enlightening discussion of the way Milton's poetry works in *Paradise Lost*.

Margaret Olofson Thickstun, *Milton's Paradise Lost: Moral Education* (Palgrave Macmillan, 2007). As the title suggests, an account of *Paradise Lost* aimed at students and addressing "the issues of self-determination and personal responsibility that they face in their lives: peer pressure, sexual desire, the pursuit of happiness, the choice of life work".

A.J.A. Waldock, *Paradise Lost and Its Critics* (Cambridge University Press, 1947). An immensely stimulating study of the state of play of Milton criticism at the mid-point of the 20th century.

Julia M. Walker (ed.), *Milton and the Idea of Woman* (University of Illinois Press, 1988). Latter 20th-century gender studies ranging over Milton's output both before and after *Paradise Lost*.

GREENWICH EXCHANGE BOOKS

STUDENT GUIDE LITERARY SERIES

The Greenwich Exchange Student Guide Literary Series is a collection of essays on major or contemporary serious writers in English and selected European languages. The series is for the student, the teacher and the 'common reader' and is an ideal resource for libraries. The *Times Educational Supplement* praised these books, saying, "The style of [this series] has a pressure of meaning behind it. Readers should learn from that ... If art is about selection, perception and taste, then this is it."

The series includes:
Antonin Artaud by Lee Jamieson (978-1-871551-98-3)
W.H. Auden by Stephen Wade (978-1-871551-36-5)
Jane Austen by Pat Levy (978-1-871551-89-1)
Honoré de Balzac by Wendy Mercer (978-1-871551-48-8)
Louis de Bernières by Rob Spence (978-1-906075-13-2)
William Blake by Peter Davies (978-1-871551-27-3)
The Brontës by Peter Davies (978-1-871551-24-2)
Robert Browning by John Lucas (978-1-871551-59-4)
Lord Byron by Andrew Keanie (978-1-871551-83-9)
Samuel Taylor Coleridge by Andrew Keanie (978-1-871551-64-8)
Joseph Conrad by Martin Seymour-Smith (978-1-871551-18-1)
William Cowper by Michael Thorn (978-1-871551-25-9)
Charles Dickens by Robert Giddings (987-1-871551-26-6)
Emily Dickinson by Marnie Pomeroy (978-1-871551-68-6)
John Donne by Sean Haldane (978-1-871551-23-5)
Elizabethan Love Poets by John Greening (978-1-906075-52-1)
Ford Madox Ford by Anthony Fowles (978-1-871551-63-1)
Sigmund Freud by Stephen Wilson (978-1-906075-30-9)
The Stagecraft of Brian Friel by David Grant (978-1-871551-74-7)
Robert Frost by Warren Hope (978-1-871551-70-9)
Patrick Hamilton by John Harding (978-1-871551-99-0)
Thomas Hardy by Sean Haldane (978-1-871551-33-4)
Seamus Heaney by Warren Hope (978-1-871551-37-2)
Joseph Heller by Anthony Fowles (978-1-871551-84-6)

George Herbert By Neil Curry & Natasha Curry (978-1-906075-40-8)
Gerard Manley Hopkins by Sean Sheehan (978-1-871551-77-8)
James Joyce by Michael Murphy (978-1-871551-73-0)
Philip Larkin by Warren Hope (978-1-871551-35-8)
Laughter in the Dark – The Plays of Joe Orton by Arthur Burke (978-1-871551-56-3)
George Orwell by Warren Hope (978-1-871551-42-6)
Sylvia Plath by Marnie Pomeroy (978-1-871551-88-4)
Poets of the First World War by John Greening (978-1-871551-79-2)
Alexander Pope by Neil Curry (978-1-906075-23-1)
Philip Roth by Paul McDonald (978-1-871551-72-3)
Shakespeare's *A Midsummer Night's Dream* by Matt Simpson (978-1-871551-90-7)
Shakespeare's *As You Like It* by Matt Simpson (978-1-906075-46-0)
Shakespeare's *Hamlet* by Peter Davies (978-1-906075-12-5)
Shakespeare's *Julius Caesar* by Matt Simpson (978-1-906075-37-8)
Shakespeare's *King Lear* by Peter Davies (978-1-871551-95-2)
Shakespeare's *Macbeth* by Matt Simpson (978-1-871551-69-3)
Shakespeare's *The Merchant of Venice* by Alan Ablewhite (978-1-871551-96-9)
Shakespeare's *Much Ado About Nothing* by Matt Simpson (978-1-906075-01-9)
Shakespeare's Non-Dramatic Poetry by Martin Seymour-Smith (978-1-871551-22-8)
Shakespeare's *Othello* by Matt Simpson (978-1-871551-71-6)
Shakespeare's *Romeo and Juliet* by Matt Simpson (978-1-906075-17-0)
Shakespeare's Second Tetralogy: *Richard II–Henry V*
  by John Lucas (978-1-871551-97-6)
Shakespeare's Sonnets by Martin Seymour-Smith (978-1-871551-38-9)
Shakespeare's *The Tempest* by Matt Simpson (978-1-871551-75-4)
Shakespeare's *Twelfth Night* by Matt Simpson (978-1-871551-86-0)
Shakespeare's *The Winter's Tale* by John Lucas (978-1-871551-80-8)
Tobias Smollett by Robert Giddings (978-1-871551-21-1)
Alfred, Lord Tennyson by Michael Thorn (978-1-871551-20-4)
Dylan Thomas by Peter Davies (978-1-871551-78-5)
William Wordsworth by Andrew Keanie (978-1-871551-57-0)
W.B. Yeats by John Greening (978-1-871551-34-1)

FOCUS Series (ISBN prefix 978-1-906075 applies to all the following titles)
James Baldwin: *Go Tell It on the Mountain* by Neil Root (44-6)
William Blake: *Songs of Innocence and Experience* by Matt Simpson (26-2)
Emily Brontë: *Wuthering Heights* by Matt Simpson (10-1)
Angela Carter: *The Bloody Chamber and Other Stories* by Angela Topping (25-5)
George Eliot: *Middlemarch* by John Axon (06-4)
T.S. Eliot: *The Waste Land* by Matt Simpson (09-5)
F. Scott Fitzgerald: *The Great Gatsby* by Peter Davies (29-3)

Michael Frayn: *Spies* by Angela Topping (08-8)
Thomas Hardy: *Poems of 1912–13* by John Greening (04-0)
Thomas Hardy: *Tess of the D'Urbervilles* by Philip McCarthy (45-3)
The Poetry of Tony Harrison by Sean Sheehan (15-6)
The Poetry of Ted Hughes by John Greening (05-7)
Aldous Huxley: *Brave New World* by Neil Root (41-5)
James Joyce: *A Portrait of the Artist as a Young Man* by Matt Simpson (07-1)
John Keats: *Isabella; or, the Pot of Basil, The Eve of St Agnes,*
   Lamia and *La Belle Dame sans Merci* by Andrew Keanie (27-9)
Harold Pinter by Lee Jamieson (16-3)
Jean Rhys: *Wide Sargasso Sea* by Anthony Fowles (34-7)
Edward Thomas by John Greening (28-6)
Wordsworth and Coleridge: *Lyrical Ballads* **(1798)** by Andrew Keanie (20-0)

Other subjects covered by Greenwich Exchange books
Biography
Education
Philosophy